A Citizen Legislature

ERNEST CALLENBACH
and
MICHAEL PHILLIPS

BANYAN TREE BOOKS/CLEAR GLASS
Berkeley/Bodega, California

© 1985 by Ernest Callenbach and Michael Phillips

A copublication of Banyan Tree Books, Berkeley,
California, and Clear Glass, Bodega, California

Bookstore orders:
Bookpeople, 2929 Fifth Street, Berkeley, CA 94710.
Telephone (415) 549-3030

Individual orders:
Clear Glass, Box 257, Bodega, CA 94922

Library of Congress Cataloging in Publication Data:

Callenbach, Ernest.
  A citizen legislature.
  1. Representative government and representation—
United States.   2. Political participation—United
States.   3. Democracy.   I. Phillips, Michael, l938-
II. Title.
JF1059.U6C35   1985   328'.3042'0973   84-28377
ISBN 0-9604320-5-1

Printed in U.S.A.

10   9   8   7   6   5   4   3   2   1

Contents

1. The Founders' Ideal: The Legislature as a Transcript of the People

At the birth of the American republic, as James Madison noted, members of the constitutional convention "wished for vigor in the government, but . . . wished that vigorous authority to flow immediately from the legitimate source of all authority. The government ought to possess not only, first, the force, but secondly, the mind or sense of the people at large. The legislature ought to be the most exact transcript of the whole society." And John Adams argued that a legislature "should be an exact portrait, in miniature, of the people at large, as it should think, feel, reason, and act like them."

This concept of a popular legislature has a deep and lasting appeal. It offers a durable standard by which to judge the composition (and the actions) of any legislature in a country which professes to live by democratic principles.

Under the conditions of mass industrial societies, however, supposedly representative bodies have diverged strikingly from this ideal. Indeed, we now take it for granted that legislative bodies are inevitably dominated by powerful interest groups. We assume without a second thought that the voice of the public at large will be heard faintly, if at all, in the jostling for power and privilege which occupies most of the time and energies of our legislatures. It is considered normal for a democracy that the attention of legislators can only be gained by careful organizing and devoted commitment by thousands of people who manage to obtain massive financing and mobilize expensive lobbying and public relations expertise—even when they are pressing views that command lasting majorities in public opinion.

Accepting such a situation as permanent is both too pessimistic and a betrayal of democratic ideals. The voice of the people ought not to be one small and financially disadvantaged voice in the national political dialogue. It should be heard in its natural majesty—clearly, forcefully, continually and automatically. This book proposes a simple, straightforward means to achieve this, within the American system of constitutional checks and balances, in one branch of our government. Grasping this possibility requires us to dare to conceive, with the founders, that a people may indeed be directly self-governing.

As it happens, we can now provide, through scientific statistical methods, a precise operational method for carrying out the founders' ideal. It is based on the earliest democratic practices evolved in Western civilization. It avoids vexing problems posed by geographic notions of representation. And it gives promise of lasting redress against abuses of the electoral process that are chronic in a society dominated by money.

The founders knew no way to achieve a "transcript" of the people except through elections. They seem not to have known of the Greek use of random selection, or "sortition," in choosing representatives, and in any case statistical procedures did not yet exist that would permit reliably representative selection by lot in a society even as populous as the original thirteen states. It is open to doubt, of course, whether so cautiously elitist a group as the founders would have seriously entertained the possibility that a legislative body could literally be drawn directly from the people at large; when they thought of "the whole society," they tended to mean propertied white males, and much of Federalist doctrine speaks to the desirability of a government's reflecting the stabilizing role of "influential persons." Our circumstances today, however, make it not only possible but essential to rethink the foundations of our electoral system, and to contemplate the possibility of achieving a transcript that would enhance democratic representation.

Our present legislatures certainly cannot be described in terms of a "transcript of the whole society"; by that test they are hopelessly *un*representative. Women, to take the most striking disparity first, constitute 51% of the adult population but comprise only 4.8% of the present House of Representatives. Blacks, 12% of the population, comprise only 4.5% of the House; Spanish-speaking persons, 6% of the population, are similarly underrepresented with 2.5% of the House. About half of the electorate, which does not vote, cannot readily be considered to be represented at all, and this group, of course, includes a vast mass of relatively disadvantaged people (something like a sixth of our population) who bear the brunt of our poverty and unemployment. Our House is comprised almost entirely of white, well-to-do males—an enormous disproportion of them lawyers (46% in 1983, though lawyers make up only a tiny fraction of our population). We thus have our own form of "taxation without representation." Taxation heavy enough to support not only the machinery of the welfare state but also a massive war machine and extensive internal and foreign police and intelligence agencies is ratified by an electoral body which represents the people at large only in a formalistic sense.

The fiction that this narrow and exclusive body "represents" the American people rests on the implicit assumption that the electorate is politically identical with the citizenry. This assumption, however, does not fit the conditions of modern American life. A small and diminishing fraction of the citizenry has real representation, for a variety of reasons we will explore below. The result is a persistent and growing gulf between the views of the people at large and the actions of their supposed

3

representatives. In recent years, for example, though stable popular majorities have existed in favor of the Equal Rights Amendment, can- and bottle-recycling, heavier expenditures on clean air and clean water, avoidance of foreign military involvement, and many other issues, our legislatures have remained unresponsive.

There is no consensus among either social scientists or politicians as to why only about half of the American eligible electorate actually votes. In any event, we fill offices in this country by the votes of surprisingly small sectors of the population, even in hotly contested presidential elections. And in non-presidential election years, voter turnouts are markedly smaller, often below 45%, with turnouts generally smaller the further down toward the local level. (The exceptions tend to be hard-fought mayoral elections and elections focused on tax issues—which seem to concern us as passionately as they did the rebellious colonists.) Thus it is not only the President and Congress, but all legislative bodies in the country, which are continued in office with the voting support of small minorities of the population at large. The fate of the country, and of its collective purse, routinely turns upon the decisions of officials who have received votes from only some 20% to 30% of the people.

This narrow political base in turn has a precarious logical base. Recent theories of representation tend to hold that an ideal representative acts in his constituents' real and long-term interest (which may sometimes be different from their expressed wishes) and deploys his accumulated political wisdom on their behalf. However, a geographic constituency has no simple or uniform interests, but rather a welter of conflicting interests. Representing all or even a sizable proportion of them is a logically impossible task; no representative, however noble or intelligent, can argue, deliberate, bargain or vote as if he were several hundred thousand people.

The current usual escape from this dilemma is to argue that the representative then must seek to serve *national* interests—even if at the cost of a majority of his immediate constituents. What this generally means in practice, however, is that unless there is overwhelming popular pressure for some measure, a legislator's acts tend to be influenced primarily by his campaign funding sources; on a wide range of questions our actual non-ideal representatives ignore the known wishes (not to mention interests) of both their constituencies and the national population, on substantial issues and for substantial periods of time.

2. The Present Electoral System Is Unrepresentative and Promotes Corruption

The representativeness of the Congress has surfaced as an acute and immediate issue in recent years because of the immense inflation of campaign expenditures. As Elizabeth Drew showed in her book *Politics and Money: The New Road to Corruption* (New York: Macmillan, 1983), the influence of campaign contributions in our national politics has become all-pervasive. Legislators are not visibly for sale, in the old nineteenth-century way, though they do hold fund-raising events at which it is made clear that they are open to the influence of money. But a kind of arms race for contributions has arisen, leading to what Rep. Jim Leach (R., Iowa) calls "a breakdown in citizen access." Or, in the fine distinction Rep. Tony Coelho (D., Calif.) attempted to make for Drew, "We don't sell legislation, we sell the opportunity to be heard." Justin Dart, presidential confidant and major fund-raiser, put it more bluntly: dialogue with politicians "is a fine thing, but with a little money they hear you better." In a long and carefully documented section of her book, Drew shows how party position-taking and Congressional maneuvering are handled with an eye to fundraising—even on bills of critical national importance, such as the 1981 tax bill, over which an open contribution "bidding war" took place. Ex-Congressmembers, when surveyed by the Center for Responsive Politics, were equally critical; according to Alvin O'Konsky (formerly R., Wisconsin), lawmakers "are bought, sold, signed, sealed and delivered by contributions before election, making them immobile to act on anything."

It is not only that the campaign funding system causes representatives to tilt toward the particular interests of major contributors, and to operate, more subtly and generally, as the representatives of the moneyed elite as a whole. Lobbyists *do* come into Congressional offices directly asking for votes for "little technical provisions" which could gain their clients millions of dollars. In many such cases the effects may be concealed. Sometimes, however, they are blatant. In 1982, the used-car dealers turned around a law requiring the listing of known defects in cars by the judicious distribution of only $675,000. In 1983, the dairy interests managed to sustain a subsidy program through votes that, in non-dairy districts, had clearly been bought by extensive campaign contributions. As an analysis by the organization Congress Watch recently showed, representatives who received large sums from chemical-company PACs favored a mild version of the Superfund toxics clean-up bill, while representatives who had received less money favored a stronger bill. Bills with backing from big contributors routinely sail through Congress with virtually no discussion, much less challenge. The shipping industry got itself largely exempted from antitrust laws in 1982, by a House vote of 350-33 (this bill was blocked in the Senate). Bills to give monopolies to brewers, bills to treat bankrupt citizens more harshly, and many other narrowly special-interest bills are adopted without scruple. On the other hand, as Drew also shows, moneyed interests can paralyze Congress into inaction on bills they dislike. "If you raise enough money, you can keep [Congress] from doing anything," one lobbyist concludes.

The influence of Washington's 20,000 lobbyists (most of them employed by corporate groups) has become so blatant that they now line up outside the House and Senate chambers giving thumbs-up or thumbs-down signals on bills as Congressmembers rush in for quick roll-call votes. (This spectacle, as Gregg Easterbrook notes in his thoughtful article "What's Wrong with Congress?" [*The Atlantic,* December 1984], is kept from the national eye by forbidding photographers to take pictures near the chamber doors.)

The result is what Drew calls a "special interest state." She is a cautious critic, but she summarizes the situation thus: "A candidate entering politics now must systematically make the rounds of the interest groups and win their approval, and their money, by declaring himself, usually in very specific terms, in favor of the legislative goals they seek. He is therefore imprisoned before he even reaches Congress. Once there, he must worry about maintaining the groups' support or about finding other groups to support him, or about casting some vote that might cause monetary retaliation. He must measure every action in terms of what the financial consequences to himself might be. The difference between that and corruption is unclear." Or, as Easterbrook concludes, "Congressmen now owe their first loyalty to PAC interests rather than to party or public interests."

The precise terminology is debatable. What is not debatable is that the present American Congress is directly controlled by moneyed interests, and that it represents, in both the political and statistical senses, only a small and shrinking segment of American society. (A similar pattern prevails in state elections, and at the county level, where contributions from developers are an overwhelming force.) This is not what Madison, Hamilton and Jay and their Federalist friends had in mind.

The founders could not have foreseen the growth of enormous concentrations of corporate wealth and power, and the parallel growth of a huge federal establishment ostensibly serving to regulate the corporate sector but in fact mostly coordinating, subsidizing, and administering it, supported by taxes on personal as well as business income. In our times, Congress has steadily shifted the tax burden from an approximately 50/50 share between corporations and individuals at the end of World War II to the present situation where, as a result of both general policy and generous provision of loopholes, only some 10% of total taxes weigh on corporations. Moreover, though in theory high incomes are taxed more heavily, compensating features of the tax code create the surprising result that in fact almost all citizens pay close to the same percentage of taxes— the millionaire and the average wage earner alike.

The conclusion is hardly far-fetched, then, whether corporate influence is being exercised through direct or indirect means: our existing Congress is not showing the concern for the interests of the citizenry upon which the founders counted to provide justice and stability for the republic. Congress is, instead, exercising the power of the public purse—which the Federalists correctly considered the fundamental power of the people, upon which all other rights depend—irresponsibly and unfairly. Almost half the people are being taxed, regulated, policed, and subjected to the possibility of nuclear annihilation without representation.

In such a serious situation, serious remedies deserve consideration. If our representatives as presently chosen are not serving their intended function, citizens must begin thinking about alternative institutions.

3. The Democracy of Athens Offers a Better Model: Selection by Lottery

It happens that there is an easy and even inexpensive way to choose representatives for a legislative body so that they would in fact be a "transcript" of the whole society: *sortition*, or selection by lottery, which was used by the Athenians to choose representatives for two centuries. The time has come to examine this type of direct representation as a possible way to bring the whole people's voice to Washington.

We have changed our notions of what constitutes proper representation many times in American history. Voting rights in the original thirteen states could be exercised only by free, white, propertied men; it was not until 1860 that property requirements were generally struck down, and in the form of poll taxes they persisted in some states until 1965. Freed black slaves theoretically received the vote in 1870. Women were not given the right to vote until 1920. The Voting Rights Act, which provided effective access to the ballot for blacks, came only in 1965. Eighteen-year-olds have voted only since 1971. It is well within the power of the American people, acting either through the amendment process or through a constitutional convention (especially if one should be called to consider the proposed balanced budget amendment) to revise our method of selecting representatives.

To put this possibility into a historical perspective, let us first consider the Athenian precedent. The *boule* or council was probably founded by Solon, the great Athenian law-giver; it was remodeled about 508 B.C. by Cleisthenes. The *boule* had judicial functions in addition to being, as representative of the periodic assembly of all citizens, generally responsible for the fiscal well-being of Athens. It had 500 members, who were paid for attendance, chosen by lottery from the ten "tribes" of

Athens to serve one-year terms; a standing chairmanship committee also rotated (by lot) among these ten tribes. *Boule* members cross-examined their chosen successors before approving them for appointment; reasons for disbarment included military service to another state, desertion from the army, squandering one's inheritance, maltreatment of one's parents, and prostitution. They could, if chance selected them again, serve a second term, but no more. Their meetings were open to the public, and nonmembers could also speak to the body. The *boule*'s scrutiny of working officialdom was persistent (it met daily) and intense. As the classicist P. J. Rhodes puts it, "The Athenian democrats in their heyday believed very firmly that experts should be answerable to the people, and subjected their activities [including their financial accounts] to close scrutiny." Aristotle called a *boule* "a characteristic organ of democracy," and all other Greek authorities regarded sortition as an essential means of equalizing the chances of rich and poor to influence government. The *boule* system prevailed for about as long as the American republic has, and lost its power only through the growth of a class of specialized officials serving long terms: in modern parlance, a bureaucracy.

Benjamin Barber, a professor of political science at Rutgers, argues in his new book *Strong Democracy* (University of California Press, 1984) for a variety of democracy-enhancing measures, including sortition for local government positions. As Barber notes, in the eighteenth century Montesquieu still took it for granted that suffrage by lot is natural to democracy. Barber has also discovered that sortition was employed briefly in the constitutions of Venice, Florence, and one canton of Switzerland. (It was also the normal method of choosing leaders in Basque communities, until the King of Spain stopped the practice.) Barber remarks that sortition has persisted to this day in the Anglo-American system of choosing juries; and as it turns out, the process of compiling prospective juror names could easily be adapted to choosing legislators by lot under modern conditions.

Just as the Athenian *boule* existed in conjunction with the citizen assembly, we may imagine a new direct-representation house of Congress existing in conjunction with a Senate chosen by traditional electoral means. In the history of Western legislatures, bodies representing wealth and privilege have often been called Senates; let us therefore preserve that name for our electoral body and suppose that its elections would remain dominated, as are those of the present Congress, by corporate campaign funds and moneyed interests generally. The new body we propose to call the Representative House. As we will explain in more detail below, three-year overlapping terms would give the new House continuity and stability. Both houses of the legislature could originate bills, as at present. (Presumably the executive would, in reality, continue to originate money bills through partisans in the House, but since origination is no longer a matter of real procedural consequence, the Senate might also be given this symbolic power.) The consent of both houses would be required for passage of bills; provisions for overriding presidential vetoes and instituting constitutional amendments would remain as they now stand.

The machinery for choosing the 435 members of the new House by sortition would be simple, inexpensive, and easy to make tamper-proof. Each county in the country already maintains a jury commission to provide lists of potential jurors to its courts. Originally such lists were drawn from the registry of voters, but in recent years potential juror lists have also included names from additional sources less likely to be biased toward the white and middle-class: driver-license lists, telephone directories, and so on. Combining all these county lists into one master national list would thus provide a virtually complete roster of eligible persons. (Just as certain categories of people are excluded from juries and the present House, some would be excluded from service in the Representative House: those under age, convicted felons, institutionalized persons, non-citizen residents.)

From this master list, elementary statistical procedures on a computer can achieve a demonstrably random selection of 435 names. This selection process can be carried out using identification numbers so that no connection between names and numbers was known to the administrating staff until the drawing had been completed. We will return to the financial implications of this system in more detail later, but it should be noted here that it would be much simpler and less expensive than our present electoral machinery; since it uses existing jury lists, it would require no new bureaucracy.

The connection with the jury system is more than mere convenience. Our attachment to judgment by a jury of our peers goes far back in British history. Especially in cases where punishment could be severe, we do not trust to elected or appointed judges. When life is possibly to be taken away, or freedom forfeited, we prefer to have judgment rendered by a body representative, in principle, of the community. In practice, this ideal is often compromised: potential juror panels are now usually quite fairly chosen, but jury commissions (and judges presiding over jury selection) are often lenient to upper-income and professional people pleading hardship. The strategic challenges allowed to attorneys further distort the representativeness of juries. Despite such limitations, however, the jury process remains a solemn and respected one. The gravity of their responsibility bears heavily upon jurors, as anyone who has served on a jury can attest, and jury deliberations are normally thorough, cautious, and serious. While few jurors are eager to serve on another jury in a hurry, most believe they have done their best, individually and collectively, to ensure that justice was done within the terms of the law.

Often, they experience new feelings of respect and attachment for the democratic process as a whole. We believe that persons chosen for a direct-representation legislature would have similar attitudes and carry out their responsibilities toward proposed legislation much as jurors carry out theirs toward alleged crimes.

4. Direct Representation Is Scientifically Reliable

Drawing jurors or representatives by "random sampling" is not haphazard, as the term leads some to think, but in fact exquisitely systematic; its accuracy is attested to by elaborate and universally accepted mathematical theory. The principle involved arises in court cases, and Dr. Peter Sherrill, who is often called upon to testify before judges and juries, finds it effective to remind them that we all use sampling in daily life. If we want to know what a pot of soup tastes like, we carefully stir the entire pot to make sure that we get the parts that settle to the bottom; most judges and juries understand that this stirring is the same as randomizing. Taking all the names of American adults, numbering them, and thoroughly mixing the numbers is comparable to stirring the soup. People can also understand readily that a spoonful is enough to test a soup whether we are dealing with a pot containing four bowls or a ship's 50-gallon kettle; the accuracy of the taste test depends not on the size of the kettle but on how thoroughly the soup is stirred.

In the case of a pot of thick soup where we wish to know its components, we do not have to sieve them all out laboriously to know how many peas, beans, and pieces of tomato and onion there are in the soup. Instead, we stir the pot carefully to make sure the ingredients are randomly distributed, and then take out a ladle full. We need only see what is in the ladle to know the proportions in the pot as a whole. A ladle full will be a very reliable measure, and for the Representative House a ladle containing 435 people would be large enough to provide the "transcript" of the nation that we are seeking.

5. A Cross-Section of the People Would Be Selected

A Representative House would be astonishingly different from its predecessors. Upon entering the House chamber you would see at work a body whose members comprise more than 50% women and some 12% blacks, 6% Hispanics, and 1% persons of other races. Because of their dress and manner, your overwhelming impression would be of middle- and working-class people. Gone would be such arch, gentlemen's-agreement phrases as, "Will the honorable member yield?" In their place would be the direct, homely idioms of the American people. "The learned member from Nebraska seems to have forgotten the morning's testimony" would give way to "What's the matter, you asleep this morning?" About a quarter of the body would be blue-collar workers, some of them accustomed to the rigors of debate in community meetings and union halls. You might try to pick out, scattered around the chamber, the ten percent who had been unemployed when their number came up: laid-off laborers, seamstresses, cooks, teamsters, seamen, secretaries, clerks. You might find it easier to spot the two doctors or dentists, the one school administrator, the two accountants, and the one real estate agent whom chance would bring to the body most years. There would also be several dozen managers and administrators dressed in upper-middle-class style. But no air of privilege would prevail

14

here. Looking around at the faces, you would see hundreds of ordinary working people, the "average Americans" who mainly make up this country. Few would be expensively groomed. Most would have the kind of faces you see in jury boxes.

You would not, most years, find more than one or two lawyers, and most of the members would have quite modest incomes. Less than 5% of the members would be as rich as the average present Congressmember. The median per capita income would be about $11,500 for women and $19,000 for men. Only 30 of the people around you would make more than $50,000 per year.

As in a jury, natural leadership qualities would assert themselves in a Representative House, sometimes for good and sometimes for ill. Who, you might wonder, are these people who are speaking to the body? Is the current speaker, delivering a passionate speech about an education bill, perhaps one of the eight teachers likely to be in the body, or is she the one school administrator? Or is she perhaps the one scientist we might expect to have? Or could she be one of our four bookkeepers, or one of our nine food service workers, or perhaps our one childcare worker? Or is she among the fully one third of the body made up of non-employed persons—retired people, housewives, students—and perhaps speaking as a parent?

And as to those who rise to question or answer her—among them might be our three carpenters, our four farm laborers, our three auto mechanics, our firefighter or our computer specialist. Who on the floor will prove the most concerned with tax-payer issues, or military issues, or health and welfare issues? Though roughly 45% of the members are nominal Democrats, something like 40% Republicans, and 15% independents, they owe nothing to their parties. The discipline of party positions, seldom an overwhelming force in American politics, is hardly apparent at all here; members do not seem to

15

be identified so much by party as by interests in specific issues. Even the region of the country they happen to come from is not of major importance—though there would be proportionately more members from the heavily populated states than from less inhabited ones, more urban than rural members, and so on.

In their infinite variety, the members of a Representative House represent comprehensively every class, every ethnic group, every political complexion. A sample of 435 persons has what is known as a margin of probable error of $\pm 2.5\%$. This means that most of the time deviations from precise representativeness would be very small, though larger deviations would occasionally occur. If the actual proportion of women in the adult population is 51%, for example, the number of women actually sent to Washington would in almost all years be between 211 and 233; it might sometimes dip or rise a little further, but the chance of it dropping to anywhere near the present level even for one year is infinitesimally small. And on the average, over a decade or so, the proportion of women in the House would be very close to 51%.

Indeed, because our sample size of 435 is a comfortably large one, we would usually find represented all attributes that occur in more than about 400,000 people. Hence we would have several vegetarians, a few people who cannot drive cars, a couple of campers and hikers; there would even usually be a Buddhist, since America now has about a half million Buddhists. Even attributes that occur in less than 400,000 people would occasionally be represented. Thus, where our present process of selecting candidates and financing campaigns eliminates not only persons with views uncongenial to moneyed backers but also persons with non-majority views of virtually any type, the sortition process would by comparison provide much more wide-ranging representation of all those political positions, and economic and political views, which are held by significant numbers of Americans. It would provide, in short, the transcript or portrait of which the founders dreamed. Hence its members would not have to agonize over whom they were representing; their statistical constituencies would simply consist of people like themselves. Their representativeness would be automatic and ineluctable. Thus their debates and decision-making would provide what democratic theorists of representation have always sought: a simulacrum of what the entire people would engage in if its members were not too numerous to be assembled.

6. A Representative House Would Frame Political Issues in New Ways

Some actions of such a House might gladden the hearts of liberals, while others would bring cheer to conservatives. It is unlikely that the body would pursue a class-conscious agenda with the singlemindedness that the ruling elite might fear; the American people have a long record of supporting measures and politicians that are, as the phrase goes, "objectively opposed" to their own material interests. Moreover, the corporate-controlled media would presumably continue to exert considerable control over the national political agenda.

It is, however, irresistible to speculate that the social composition of the new House might cause it to see certain types of issues differently than the current House. Legislative oversight of federal expenditures might be rather more intense than at present. When issues such as deregulation came up, considerations of service to communities or to the people as a whole might loom larger than devotion to pure ideals of free enterprise. Americans have always been attached to the dream of individuals making it big by their own efforts, and reluctant to endorse measures that would bring about greater economic equality, but a direct-representation House might seek to make the tax system at least slightly progressive. (Only a third of Americans believe the current tax system is fair; in this they join former president Carter, who called it "a disgrace.") And the new House might be sympathetic to other means of redressing the severe (and growing) inequities in American income.

Judging by many soundings of American public opinion, whatever their incomes or work roles, most members would consider themselves middle-class and moderate. At least before being exposed to debate on the issues, only a weak majority, if that, would defend free speech for both "leftists" and "rightists." (This is not notably worse than elected legislatures traditionally do, however; it has always been the courts that defend civil liberties against the assaults of the legislature and the executive.) There would be solid majorities against school bussing and open housing to achieve racial integration; about a third would even favor laws prohibiting racial intermarriage, and more than 40% would also like to outlaw homosexuality. More than two thirds would favor legal abortion—and also the allowing of prayer in public schools. On economic matters, rather like members of the present House, they would initially favor a contradictory combination of more spending and lower taxes. By a considerable margin they would favor a nuclear weapons freeze and some buildup of conventional armaments. A large majority would be in favor of the death penalty.

While such matters are harder to predict, the new House would probably display special concern over national health insurance policies, housing conditions, unemployment, business fraud, and bureaucratic red tape where it affects ordinary citizens. It might well insist on stricter controls over work-related chemical exposures, on improved safety features in automobiles, and on more cautious policies regarding potential carcinogens in pesticide, herbicide, and food additive forms.

18

And it might also be more cautious than our elected House on war-related issues: almost two thirds of the American people object to committing troops overseas except in the case of a direct attack on the country.

Such views on the part of the new House members would be welcome to some and unwelcome to others, but it is hard to believe they would not command respect from the populace. Living by the considered will of the people is what democracy is supposed to be about. We no longer have to settle for a deformed simulacrum of the people, achieved through a corrupted electoral process. The immediacy of direct democracy, ordinarily thought impossible in a numerous society, is paradoxically now within our practical grasp.

The moral authority of a Representative House would introduce a new dynamic into the political process. Just as a newly elected president brings to Washington a sense of mandate from the electorate, which can often result in an effective initial legislative thrust, the members of the new House would bring with them a new vitality and urgency, drawn from the roots of America. If this House says "No" to the president or the Senate, its impact will be great, for such a negative would not merely be the resultant of Congressional wrangling, but the expression of the people. A proposed policy which had been refused by the House could not expect to be sneaked through next year; its passage would have to await extended discussion and change of views on the part of the public at large, from which each year's House would be drawn.

7. A Representative House Would Restore the Difference Between the House and Senate

If a Representative House were established, there might be an initial period in which its role would be chiefly to review and either approve or reject bills originated by the Senate. Members of the Senate, elected with the support of the country's corporate interests—which are, under today's conditions, interpenetrated with the Pentagon and other sections of the bureaucracy—would presumably remain active in proposing bills which favor their de facto constituents. Bills aimed at serving the general welfare would also presumably originate from the Senate from time to time, since its members would still have to pass periodic tests of general election.

However, as the role of the new House became more familiar, and as it developed its own staff support services and traditions, it would surely begin to generate substantial numbers of bills. Following in the great tradition of American legislatures, each body would check and balance the other through the familiar process of horse-trading. If the Senate wished to pass a new armaments bill to enrich corporate suppliers, it might have to agree to the passage of a House bill enforcing consumer protections; if the House wished to pass a bill to ensure clean drinking water, it might have to agree to a bill allowing additional corporate tax loopholes. A Representative House is not a utopian scheme that would completely overhaul Washington. But what it *can* deliver is worth thinking about: one half of a government that would truly be "of the people, by the people, and for the people."

This kind of pragmatic bicameralism fits in well with the history of American representative institutions. We have never had legislative houses with explicitly different class bases, as has been the case in Britain where the House of Lords is made up of hereditary nobles, and the House of Commons of ordinary citizens. (It is only recently that the Lords have lost all their powers; in the past century they were still the dominant house.) The American Senate, whose members until 1920 were chosen by the state legislatures rather than by the voters at large, is sometimes considered a more august body than the House; its members are somewhat richer on average, and the Senate possesses powers over executive appointments and treaties which the House lacks. Senators do not, however, remain in office notably longer than members of the House. (Fifty percent of the House stays in office more than six years; 52% of the Senate stays more than six years. Interestingly enough, there has been a steady decline in reelection of Congressional incumbents: from 86% in 1956 down to 55% in 1980.) And because of the intricate linkages among members of the legislature, the executive bureaucracy, and the corporate world, the divisions between the two houses are often nominal; the greatest flurry of apparent opposition occurs when one house is controlled by the Democrats while the other is controlled by the Republicans, but even then substantial coordination prevails.

Adoption of a Representative House would thus reintroduce true bicamerality into the American legislative process. The ultimate sources of power of the two bodies would again be markedly different: the Senate would rely on the moneyed interests that secured its members' election, and the House would rely on its role as direct representative of the people at large. Thus, a Representative House would extend into contemporary conditions our traditional concern to limit any undue concentration of power.

8. The Representative House Would Develop Its Own Organization

When the founders contemplated the terms of office they would establish for members of the Senate and House, they were sensitive to two conflicting demands. The colonial devotion to liberty had led, as Madison put it, to the widespread belief that "where annual elections end, tyranny begins." Officials, being human, were always susceptible to corruption both monetary and political, and the only sure defense against the establishment of an exploitative oligarchy was the traditional American opportunity to throw the rascals out—which needed to be frequent and unobstructed.

On the other hand, the business of a national legislature was bound to be complex, and excessively short terms would not permit the familiarization of legislators with facts, precedents and policies that could give continuity and stability to their actions. Longer terms also serve to insulate legislators from momentary vogues in public opinion.

The first consideration predominated in the establishment of the House of Representatives, a relatively large body (100 at the time of the first census, in 1790) subject to a total reconstitution every two years. The opposing considerations found expression in the Senate, with its six-year overlapping terms and smaller membership.

In our Representative House, comprising 435 members, we could continue to combine these two kinds of considerations by setting the membership term at three years, and replacing one third of the members each year, with the same constitutional requirements as to age (25) and citizenship (seven years minimum) as at present.

This arrangement would ensure continuity from year to year; two thirds of the membership, and hence usually of the

22

leadership also, would remain in place each year. Members would reside in Washington long enough to develop familiarity with government affairs but not long enough to become fixtures. The fact that they could not remain longer (or return) would make them less attractive to potential bribery attempts, and the brevity of their terms would mean they would retain for much of their terms a vivid sense of the communities from which they came and to which they would shortly return.

Until 1975, the existing Congress was dominated by elderly and mostly conservative committee chairmen, entrenched by long seniority, who could effectively block public-interest legislation—and make or break the careers of junior members. At present, an elaborate system of committees and subcommittees has proliferated, whose main concerns often seem to be battling each other over legislative "turf" or providing media exposure useful in appealing to voters. The byzantine complications of this system offer many ways to conceal responsibility (often a prime consideration for an elected official) and in the end give greater sway to lobbyists. Starting from scratch, the Representative House could hardly fail to develop a committee structure that would be simpler, more efficient, and more responsive. It would have no motive, for instance, to separate authorizing functions from appropriation and taxing functions (a source of endless buckpassing and internal friction in the present Congress); a committee that proposed a bill could also be obliged to propose ways for paying for what it enacted, instead of pushing that problem off onto another committee.

We assume that the Representative House would establish means to initiate its new members and provide them with training and background information to enable them to carry out their new functions. At least their first three months in Washington would be spent in a total-immersion training school, which would serve the same basic purposes as do a judge's instructions to a jury, not to mention army basic training. This mini-university of politics should be among the finest educational institutions in the country. It should draw upon the best professors from our leading universities and utilize former House leaders who would return as guest instructors. The challenge of educating 145 new members each year, who would not only help guide the nation during their term but would thereafter return to their communities and presumably remain influential people, should attract the energies of many innovative educators.

The training school would acquaint new members with the traditions, regulations, and procedures of the House, and with the power relationships, formal and informal, prevailing between it and the other institutions of the federal government. It would provide in-depth background about major legislative issues likely to be acted upon in the coming months. It would give new members practice in debate and decision-making by participation in mock legislative sessions. And it would teach members the perquisites and limitations of their office—including the features of the criminal code that relate to bribery.

In any large body, the method of selection and the powers of the leadership are crucial factors, and as with the present House, these would be evolved by the body itself. Initially, since much of the agenda of the new House would originate in the Senate, the leadership's main tasks would be to arrange for fair debate. A rotating chair system, such as the Athenians employed in their *boule*, would suffice for these needs and would minimize the dangers of favoritism. But as the Representative House became an established institution and began to generate its own legislation, it would surely develop a more structured leadership and perhaps standing committees. It would probably develop factions or caucuses on various ad hoc bases, reflecting as it would the great tides of political perception and priorities of the general populace. Thus a women's caucus, black caucus, or unemployed caucus might on occasion play as important a role as the traditional parties.

In such groupings, leadership should be abundant, and it would be different from the brokering style of leadership that dominates the present Congress. Our current representatives are in fact seldom natural leaders, of the kind who spring up among people to cope with natural disasters, who are chosen as jury foremen or forewomen, who emerge in fighting groups in the military, or who arise when voluntary community associations face crises. The present House is, instead, mostly led by people whose views and actions are defined by narrow questions of legislative strategy and infighting. They are so "realistic" that they rarely can get others to follow them in changing anything. Members of a Representative House would find more dynamic leadership.

The point of politics is the articulation and peaceful mutual adjustment of conflicting interests, and this process arises in any collection of human beings, beginning with the family. Exactly how it would take shape in a Representative House no one can predict, any more than the founders could have foreseen the specific mode of operations of the existing House. But, with 435 independent and unbeholden people gathered together for the purpose of making national policy, we may be confident it would be a vigorous—and representative—process of conflict and accommodation.

9. The Representative House Would Better Serve the General Welfare

It might be objected that a Representative House with terms of only three years would possess little collective "memory" or tradition. The evil consequences feared are that the House would lack the accumulated experience needed for skillful negotiations with the Senate or the administration and that the body would not have leaders who, because they had served for lengthy periods, possessed great legislative sagacity. We feel that the first fear is a justified one, and it can be countered only by the argument that, when dealing with the members of the Representative House, senators or presidents would be encountering people over whom they had no leverage save that of argument. If we believe that a direct-representation House can deal competently with legislative debate, it seems certain that it can deal with legislative conniving.

The second fear seems, from a public viewpoint, largely groundless. If the supposed wisdom of the Congress were indeed being used in the public interest, we would not live in a country with such shamefully elevated rates of poverty, unemployment, ill-health, illiteracy, early death, etc., etc. By almost any statistical comparison with other industrial democracies, the American public is not being well protected by its legislatures; indeed it might be suspected that the political skills of those in power are being used as much against the people as for them. A body selected without the corruptions of our electoral process would thus probably display more direct and effective concern for the condition of its fellow citizens.

James Madison, writing his brilliant defense of Federalist plans for the House and Senate, summarized the requirements of good government as "first, fidelity to the object of government, which is the happiness of the people; secondly, a knowledge of the means by which that object can be best attained." As he then wryly noted, some governments are deficient in both, but most governments are deficient in the first—because the people's powers are insufficient to enforce it. The people's power to elect representatives to the existing House has been diluted by the size, media systems, and corporate domination of modern society. This critical power must now be placed back in their hands.

We have no doubt that many who first encounter the idea of a Representative House, whether they admire or despise the present Congress, will be startled and resistant to giving it serious consideration. This has always been the first reaction to proposals to extend democratic representation—proposals which, nonetheless, have sooner or later come to prevail. When the idea that women should be entitled to vote was first proposed, it was bitterly ridiculed. Nonetheless, when American women finally obtained the vote, none of the dire predictions that had been made by opponents proved accurate. Indeed, until the last two elections, no detectible difference had ever been found in the voting behavior of men and women, and the idea that women in some countries have not been allowed to vote until recently (Switzerland as late as 1971) seems ludicrous to us now.

Traditionally, people of aristocratic inclinations or positions have opposed extension of the suffrage to non-propertied persons in vociferous terms, predicting the downfall of all ordered society (not to mention the loss of their own favored status). Fortunately or unfortunately, such predictions have also proved without foundation. We suggest that initial objections to the idea of direct representation will meet the same fate.

10. The Representative House Would Be Equivalent to the Nation as a Whole

It may be objected that the Representative House, since its members would not face possible public disapproval and defeat in elections, would not be controllable by the citizenry it represented. Members would not face sanctions or serious risks by voting in one way rather than another (or by not voting at all); hence, the body's actions might be frivolous, erratic, or irresponsible.

We believe that this objection ignores the statistical significance of the random selection process. Representative House members do not have to be forced by external circumstances to represent constituents because, by the very statistics of their selection, they inevitably *do* represent their segment of the populace.

This is a difficult and critical point, one that goes to the heart of the difference between the election and sortition principles. It is precisely because elected representatives are likely to be so different from their geographical constituents (richer, whiter, mostly male) that a traditional representative system of government requires electoral checks and controls upon the representatives. But if, through sortition, the representatives statistically are a "transcript," closely equivalent to the people themselves, then this problem vanishes. The Representative House, for all practical purposes, would be identical to the people. It would have the moral force attributable to an assembly of the entire people in a small society like Athens (or a New England town).

Besides giving proper representation of direct citizen interests, a sortition House would tap the real but often eroded patriotism of the American people. Members of the present elected House are heavily constrained in their actions by obligations to financial contributors, fellow party members, administration power-holders, and organized interest groups among their constituents. The members of a sortition House would be insulated from these forces. It would thus be within their power simply to do what they saw as right for the country.

11. The Representative House Would Be at Least as Competent as the Present House

The objection may be raised that a Representative House would not be competent to deal with the complex issues of modern government. This objection reflects the feeling, which is widespread although it may not be founded in reality, that our rulers are (or at any rate should be) "better than us"—a feeling which is a major factor in the acquiescence of citizens in their own disempowerment. When we examine this objection concretely, however, it loses much substance. The election process as practiced in our media age rewards candidates who have congenial TV images, have a convincing verbal delivery, and are adept at sensing transient public emotional moods. These qualities do not necessarily correlate with either intelligence or responsible political leadership.

It is certainly not obvious, in any case, that our present representatives are really the kind of people we would ideally want to have making critical, life-and-death decisions for us. Nor is there any convincing evidence that they are superior in wisdom, judgment, compassion, and sense of responsibility to 435 people chosen by sortition from the citizenry at large. The latter would certainly have, among themselves, a livelier and more realistic sense of the life of the country and its pressing problems; they would have a more varied collective experience to draw upon, and they would not be constrained in their thinking by a desire to cosset corporations. As personalities, they would probably be on average less aggressive, greedy, and sexist. In personal morality, it is hard to believe that their peccadilloes and perversities would be greater than those revealed by the Congresses of our century.

Many features of the existing legislative process would doubtless remain in a Representative House. The drafting of laws would continue to be done by executive employees, legislative analysts, business lobbyists, and citizen organizations, working with Congressional staff members. The Congressional research staff would continue to produce analytic studies, hearings would provide expert testimony, and so on. A Representative House might avail itself routinely of analyses similar to those which describe and evaluate the effects of initiative measures in the voter booklets of some states.

But actual bills would probably look rather different, and they would probably be fewer in number. As Irving Younger has argued, it is actually scandalous that Congress passed 3,359 laws from 1970-79, and he proposed several standards which might also appeal to a citizen House. The first is: "Congress may not vote on a bill unless a majority of the legislators present have read it." (Senator Daniel Moynihan, D., N.Y., has in fact introduced a bill to that effect.) The second is: "No law may be passed that is so complex that it cannot be understood by a person of reasonable intelligence exercising reasonable diligence." As Younger points out, one sentence of the Internal Revenue Code is 506 words long. This kind of protective impenetrability, which favors elements in society able to hire lawyers who can deal with it, would probably be greatly reduced by a Representative House, which could send obfuscatory legislation back for redrafting.

Much is made of the complexity of the Congressional work load, but it appears that only about 150 bills a year receive real debate. Since at present considerably more than half of a Congressmember's time and energy (and that of his or her staff) is devoted to re-election efforts and fund-raising, members tend to become dependent on staff for orientation and recommendations about bills. While Representative House members would still need expert staffs, their entire attention would be on the legislative process. Some members might be more malleable under the influence of their staffs than existing elected members, but many ordinary citizens are also stubborn and hard to manipulate; moreover, the traditional opportunist arguments about electoral appeal could not be used by staff, so some direct-representation members might prove *less* malleable than are elected members.

In passing, it is worth noticing that the way the present House deals with the work load is to sometimes pass bills en masse: just before adjournment in 1983, 200 bills were passed without discussion in one afternoon. It requires a certain elitist disdain for the citizenry to suppose that their representatives could not apply native common sense to the business of the republic, and a certain credulity to suppose that members of the present House are gifted with magical levels of political foresight. In any case, pure intelligence—if there is such a thing—is certainly not directly related to political wisdom. The only reasonable assumption is that both "pure" and political intelligence are broadly distributed through the population.

Resistance to the sortition idea comes generally, in the last analysis, from an attachment to hierarchy and a lack of trust in the people themselves. But to endorse sortition as a means of representing the people does not require believing that the people are perfect. Any town meeting, like any elected body, has a rich mixture of individuals. Some are cooperative and devoted to the common welfare, even capable of self-sacrifice. Some are venal and self-interested. Some are easy-going, some are harsh and combative. Some are quick spoken, some are slow and deliberate. Some are honest, some are devious. Some are independent minded, some are cautious or cowardly. In the tradition of the town meeting, or of the small face-to-face democratic cultures that preceded the industrial epoch, all these varied human beings met in a common place and dealt with one another, achieving the kind of agreements necessary to hold the society together in an acceptably just order. This democratic process has its irritations, its limits, its ironies. But it is, as Winston Churchill remarked, still the best system of governance humankind has yet devised, and there seems no reason why it should not be enjoyed by representatives who are truly representative.

12. The Representative House Would Be No More Easily Manipulated Than the Present House

We may ask whether the Representative House would be easily stampeded by forceful or charismatic presidents. In order to gain a perspective on this question we must look at the record of the existing House. Congressmembers have always been prone to abandon independent judgment in war-hysteria situations, and recent history offers several chilling examples of abdication of powers. The most notorious recent case, and the most costly to the nation, was when Lyndon Johnson persuaded Congress to pass the Gulf of Tonkin Resolution authorizing a de facto state of war in Vietnam. Only one senator, Wayne Morse (R., Oregon) resisted the flood of jingoism on this occasion. He issued a dire warning, which as it turned out was entirely accurate, about the probable consequences of the Congressional action; but Congress went along with the president. More recently, Congress was loath to enforce the provisions of the Wars Powers Resolution on Ronald Reagan's warlike policies in Central America.

It seems doubtful that a House drawn directly from the people would be much better or much worse in such respects than our existing House. In an increasingly media-dominated political system, with the party structures in decline, the ability of presidents to control Congress directly probably ended with Lyndon Johnson. Congress too is now a "public" for presidential initiatives, to be cajoled and persuaded, and it is perhaps additionally fitting that this role should be played by direct representatives of the people.

In an era when the costs of the Vietnam War are still remembered (50,000 dead, $430 billion), a direct-representation House might be less prone to most war enthusiasms than an elected one. War casualties come from the ranks of ordinary people; there are few lawyers in foxholes. The economic costs of war are borne by the people at large, not by the corporate figures who normally influence Congressional decision-making. Wars in distant places for objectives that cannot be made clear to the ordinary American might thus find less support in a Representative House than in the present House, whose Armed Forces Committee tends to be a Pentagon rubber stamp.

But on the other hand, if a situation should arise in which genuine national interests were clearly and directly threatened, the Pentagon might find itself backed by a supportive populace in a way unknown since World War II. And, nuclear conflict aside, the ardent support of its people is an army's greatest weapon.

13. The New House Would Be Less Corruptible than the Present House

With urban congressional campaigns costing an average of $1 million every two years, we have a "bought" Congress. To be "corrupted" presumably means that one must change the way one votes in return for favors. Under present circumstances the favors are not dollars going directly into personal pockets, but dollars making re-election possible. Corruption in the old sense is a moot point.

33

When the FBI entrapped Congressmen in the Abscam prosecution, which was a caper intended to single out the most blatantly corrupt members, the agents had to pose as Arab sheiks. Posing as an Arab sheik with an interest in buying legislation was hard to do because sheiks are not abundant in the FBI. But such a difficult cover was necessary in order to show that the "favors" the Congressmen promised could not possibly have been in the ordinary prior interests of the legislators.

In choosing Arab sheiks as their cover the FBI, in a way, admitted the corruption of the entire current electoral system. To prove their case they had to go to a ridiculous extreme.

The fundamental reason citizens dislike corruption is that it seems undemocratic. It allows special interest groups to exercise power out of proportion to their numbers. In contemporary terms it means that the American auto companies' top management, a few hundred men, are able to build unsafe cars that cause tens of thousands of needless deaths and pollute the urban air; this in turn causes death, disease, disability and property damage for more than 200 million other Americans. Corruption generally allows powerful minorities to protect their interests at the expense of many others. Democratic ideals favor protecting minority interests but without damaging others.

Many reforms have been undertaken over the past one hundred years to try to decrease the corruption of elected officials. The Corrupt Practices Act at the beginning of the twentieth century made blatant corruption, the type highlighted in Abscam, illegal. Legislation in the 1960's introduced campaign spending restrictions and required publication of donations and donors; more recently Congress has tried to limit the outside income of its members and created political action committees (PAC s) as a way to raise money from more diverse interest groups. Federally channeled funds are even being provided to presidential candidates in hopes of reducing their dependence on donors. Lobbyists are now required to publicly register on the national level.

Such reforms are of course desirable. But they do not touch the fundamental corruption that Elizabeth Drew and others have documented. This new, quiet, genteel corruption is inherent in *election* systems, because all candidates really do need money. It is not inherent in the *sortition* system, because there representatives are selected without any need for campaign money.

A Representative House is not theoretically immune to all corruption. But in practicality naive people are harder to corrupt than sophisticated ones. In theory a few highly influential members could be bribed with rewards given to their publicly unknown friends or relatives, or with promises of rewards several years after they leave office. However, requirements for disclosure of income and restraints on post-office-holding job conflicts would suffice to mitigate such potential abuses.

In practical terms it would be nearly impossible to corrupt a sortition legislature. Finding the few corruptible people would be hard, finding any small group that could influence the remaining members would be even harder, and evidence of the corruption would be easily detectible. Imagine a GM executive talking with his lobbyist. "Jim, we've got to stop the air bag legislation. It's worth $100 million to us if you can do it." "Jack, here's the problem. There are a dozen guys and two women who could be bribed with money to their relatives and with prostitutes, but only one or two of them have broad influence in the House and on this issue any of them might blow the whistle on us. If that happened we'd lose not only on the air-bag issue, but most of these people would be so mad at GM, they'd want us split into many smaller companies like AT&T."

Nor is it easy to see how the information flow to members of a Representative House could be controlled by powerful interests. The members would possess staffs capable of independent research; the national press and media, while badly compromised as sources of disinterested information by their corporate ownership, still possess some independence. And members of a Representative House, functioning as a kind of national political jury, would doubtless be flooded with information and opinion from many sources besides the "respectable" press.

14. The Members Would Be Representative Even When Absent

Among 435 citizens selected to be members of the Representative House, we should expect some small percentage of them to stay home—keep the salary that goes with their new position and just stay where they are, or possibly move to Hawaii and become beach bums.

In the present Congress there are always a few members who are sick, don't come to the office because they are drunk, take long vacations during active sessions, or spend their time on junkets. But the most frequent reason given for members not being present to vote is that they are back in their home districts campaigning. (Their expense accounts now provide for about forty trips home each year.) Two techniques are used to cover up for absent members. One is "pairing up." A member finds someone who is also going to be absent when a vote is taken and would have voted the opposite way. They then submit a "paired vote" so each can nullify the other's vote. The second is voice voting which is not recorded at all. Both of these techniques are commonly used in spite of the fact that four out of five important votes are scheduled for the convenience of members well in advance on Tuesdays, Wednesdays and

Thursdays so members can take long weekends. In addition, members can record their vote days or weeks after the actual vote, which is also permitted for absentees as long as their additional vote doesn't affect the outcome.

For the average of 520 votes per year that were recorded in the past five years 10% of the members were absent, despite advance scheduling. Some members have worse records than others. Nine Congressmembers in 1983 voted on less than 80% of the House roll calls.

Most Americans believe that governing our country is important and that our representatives should show an appropriate interest in their official duties—especially since they are well paid and many of the issues before the Congress affect the personal lives and well being of the citizens. Yet nothing has been done to ensure greater attendance. The common successful use of poor attendance as a campaign issue is proof that the electorate believes their present representatives are paid to attend sessions and vote.

The Representative House would face a similar attendance problem. It is possible that some members would only be present to vote 80% of the time and that 5% might almost never come to Washington. But it is hard to believe that many would be gone most Mondays and Fridays, as is routinely the case with the present House.

The difference is significant. Direct-representation members who stay home would be doing so because it was a free personal choice, though not a popular one. (We must remember that the identities of the chosen Representatives will be widely known in their home communities, which would not take absenteeism lightly.) But the Representative House members who don't vote will even in their non-voting be truly representative of the public on the issues before the Congress. Issues important to everyone will get high attendance, minor issues will be ignored. The same thing happens every day in PTA

37

meetings and office gatherings: a PTA meeting about committee reports may have 5% of the members present, a discussion of racially based bussing may get 90%. An office gathering to discuss pension plan modifications may get just the older employees, but planning the desk arrangements or working hours may get everyone.

Attendance in the present Congress is often to support special interests or repay obligations. In a Representative House it would almost always be some mixture of personal feelings, a sense of obligation to the common good and interest in the issue. Members who stayed at home would be those who could withstand the social pressure of their neighbors and friends; it's probably better that they stay home, since the common good is not important to them. Nevertheless there would be some issues that even they would go to vote on, where their own ox was being gored.

However, the members of the current Congress who stay away are not "representative" of the general public. The ones who go home to campaign are often the ones who won election by narrow margins. Others are out giving lectures to make money for themselves, or travelling on junkets.

The people who will be most disturbed by the absenteeism in a direct-representation legislature are those who don't know how bad the current situation is, those who have trouble understanding the nature of true representation, and those whose moral values are too narrow to encompass that fact that the work ethic is not universal in contemporary American life.

15. Campaign Funding Reforms Will Not Solve the Current Problems of Proper Representation

Some who view our present electoral practices with dismay believe that they can be reformed without resort to the remedy of a Representative House. Naive reform proposals merely propose a pious ceiling on total expenditures for the various levels of office. These would be so easy to circumvent that they require no discussion. More serious proposals involve the financing of campaigns solely by government, with no private financing permitted, so that each candidate would supposedly have exactly the same amount to spend. Proponents argue that this would give "a level playing field for ideas" (and candidates). Not surprisingly, little enthusiasm for this "extreme" proposal has arisen in Washington, most of whose political inhabitants arrived there on the strength of campaign funding as unequal as they could manage to obtain.

The organization Common Cause, which has served as a watchdog against government abuses, has proposed supplementary government financing of congressional elections, incorporating provisions to halt the abuses which have effectively nullified the intent of the similar presidential-election financing law. Support for such modest moves is reportedly growing. We wish such attempts well, but it seems probable that they will, as did the well meant provisions for political action committees (PACs), lead to new and worse abuses, while lulling the people into thinking that something has been done. Political money is a hydraulic system; if you stop up a leak in one place, the level rises and causes a break someplace else. Even the idea Elizabeth Drew advocates, that paid political advertising might be entirely prohibited and equal free air time provided, would merely send campaign funds flowing more copiously into direct mail, print ads, and doubtless other devices not yet invented. (When faced with opponents skilled in the use of the equal-time provisions of the Fairness Doctrine, moneyed interests sometimes voluntarily forego paid TV and radio time; they can win without it, given enough funds for other types of campaigning.)

Measures to provide government funding on the state or national level rest on the assumption that if candidates are provided enough money to run a decent basic campaign, their anxiety about money would be greatly diminished—and hence their temptation to court corporate (or union) interests for extra cash. It seems certain, however, that this kind of measure would simply escalate the arms race in campaign spending to new, higher levels. The U.S. Supreme Court has consistently upheld the rights of committees or individuals to spend as much on candidates as they wish. As Elizabeth Drew put it, in her quietly acid way, "The Court equated freedom of speech with the spending of money."

Thus, while electoral reforms are certainly deserving of support, and campaigns for them will always be needed, vast amounts of unidentifiable and uncontrollable money will continue to slosh around in the political system. The parties alone (not including supposedly independent "committees") spent some $300 million in the 1982 elections; one House candidate spent more than $2 million and two senators more than $7 million.

Even if the effects of such stupendous sums could be controlled to some degree in the final elections, the problems of money's influence would simply move back one notch to the primaries. And even if primary funds were also someday provided by government, the question would become how entrants were selected to run in the primaries. The ability to obtain voter signatures, a common device to select serious primary candidates, is now largely a question of money too. Modern canvassing operations, at somewhere between $1.00 and $1.50 per head, are capable of amassing signatures in almost any desired quantity for almost any measure or personality. Moneyed interests can still buy primary candidates. Voter registration campaigns, similarly, though they may well make some small contribution toward less distorted representation, depend on large-scale funding to be effective.

The conclusion seems inescapable that in a society like ours, politicians facing election campaigns will always be for sale. Electoral reform bills may do some small good; some of them might result in a slight overall drop in the amount of money society devotes to selecting its legislators. But if we really wish to have unbeholden legislators, we must break the cash link entirely. The only means available for doing that in a fair and democratic way is direct representation.

16. The Initiative Process Cannot Solve the Current Problems of Proper Representation

Even aside from the reform of electoral campaigns, could there not be other measures short of a Representative House that might bring relief from our situation? Any such possible measures certainly deserve the most serious examination.

The only significant alternative we are aware of which would seek to reach the root of our present difficulties is extension of the initiative process to the national electorate. Many state constitutions permit the people (or, under some circumstances, the legislature) to put measures on the ballot for approval or disapproval. This right is surely an essential safeguard, and it is surprising that it has been so slow to win widespread acceptance. But its effectiveness in practice has been limited, even in those states where its use is common. California voters, for example, have attempted to by-pass their reluctant legislature on the nuclear freeze, state water subsidies, bottle recycling, and the control of smoking in public places. Heavy corporate spending, however, is usually able to overturn even initial opinion odds of 3:1.

Steven D. Lydenberg of the Council on Economic Priorities has analyzed many different initiative campaigns, and he finds that grassroots organizations can indeed sometimes get proposals onto the ballot when their legislators have been unresponsive. In a few cases they have actually won—usually when aided by professional campaign people who make persistent use of the media Fairness Doctrine. However, corporate spending is able to defeat virtually all initiatives. In California since 1968, special interests have outspent opponents by more than two to one in 15 initiative campaigns; they won in 14 cases. The influence of uncontrolled and often unreported money which Elizabeth Drew documented for election campaigns is duplicated here. On issues of importance to major industrial groups, such as anti-nuclear bills, bottle bills, or smoking-control measures, proponents are outspent by opponents by huge ratios. In 1982 many state initiatives were fought with funds running to several million dollars. Even on the city level, expenditures are staggering. In 1983, tobacco interests spent $1.2 million—eight times what the proponents spent— in a not quite successful effort against a smoking-control initiative in San Francisco. (This was the first time the industry has suffered such a defeat.)

Curiously enough, although corporate spending can generally defeat initiatives, it is not highly effective in passing them. Some of this effect may be due to the prevalence of deceptive media advertising in corporate campaigns; its daring is legendary, but it may be more suitable for generating suspicion than in building support for measures. Only Oregon permits lawsuits for false political advertising—something that CEP advocates as a national necessity, and which of course would have desirable results anywhere, and in any kind of campaign.

Another abuse susceptible to remedy is that presently corporations sometimes spend as much as a million dollars on initiative campaigns—even on campaigns of no clearly direct relevance to their own business. Here, CEP is seeking Securities & Exchange Commission regulations to require reporting of such expenditures to stockholders, who presumably would put a stop to most of them.

The possibility of national initiative campaigns is attractive in principle, and it is forcefully advocated by Benjamin Barber in his case for "strong democracy." Allowing them (which would require a constitutional amendment) would provide a weapon that the people might occasionally be able to take up successfully against a somnolent or corrupt Congress. However, a number of factors would combine to make such use infrequent and likely to face defeat. Even state initiative campaigns are extremely expensive to run against the massed power of corporate wealth; financing a national campaign would be a forbidding undertaking. Volunteer citizen groups would find it daunting to coordinate a full-scale national campaign. Moreover, the most effective weapon of citizen groups, the Fairness Doctrine which provides them some access to the media, will probably soon be overturned in the rush to deregulation. It seems improbable, thus, that national initiatives could have much impact.

17. Electronic Technology Cannot Solve the Current Problems of Representation.

It is sometimes suggested that, if more direct democracy were desired in America, it could soon be achieved by a system of push-button polling in homes. Since cable TV is capable of two-way communication, issues could be debated before the viewing audience and votes could then be tabulated electronically.

Three political problems with such a system, however, seem to us insuperable. First, since there would be no physical assembly of voters, no genuinely open debate or discussion or reformulation of issues could take place. Control would remain tightly in the hands of those posing the issues at media headquarters. Moreover, possession of cable TV hookups is strongly biased by economic status, since many people cannot afford the monthly fees.

Second, this system would also exacerbate tendencies toward a kind of consumer advertising in politics. We have already come a long way from the relatively policy-oriented party organizations of the past, toward a politics of personality preferences in which people get elected for their acting talent rather than their political positions. Direct polling would tend to reduce issues to the scale of preferences for beer brands: marginal and mainly meaningless choices. The votes cast would be added up at headquarters like choices at a supermarket check stand.

The third and most crushing disadvantage of direct polling is that, as with self-selected newspaper polls, the sample of the public obtained would be highly biased in the statistical sense. Those taking an active part in the process would be self-selected. To base the fate of the nation on such a sample would clearly be folly.

18. The New House Would Save the Taxpayers Money

Sending 435 ordinary citizens to Washington D.C. to live for several years might seem expensive. Most members of the new House with families (about 33% would have only a spouse and 40% would have children) would want to bring their families and most would want to return home regularly to visit their friends.

The present House of Representatives with 435 members costs the tax payer well over $380 million per year. This does not include the cost of the new House office building which was $140 million.

Each of the current members of the House is paid $72,600 per year for salary. In addition, he or she is given an office in the home district and travel expenses, for an average cost to the taxpayers of $110,000. Each has a personal staff of 20 or more well paid people at an average of $350,000 in staff wages per House member.

The total House has 12,000 employees. In addition Representatives get free postage and send millions of pieces of mail to campaign in their home districts at a cost of $60 million per year. Overseas travel is $3 million per year.

The American people want their representatives to be reasonably taken care of and want the Congress to have a highly professional staff to match the wiles of the executive branch. But a House budget that comes to $900,000 per member does not seem to result in a particularly effective institution.

Since Congress votes its own wages, establishes its own budget, and has no known structural restraints there have been no internal budgetary reforms in the course of its history, but public resentment of recent pay raises has been intense.

A Representative House would be considerably less expensive, even if salaries were raised a bit. Since direct representatives would not need to campaign for re-election, they would not need free postage to send millions of letters to their constituencies. They would not need the half to three quarters of the current House staff which is used for fundraising and maintaining relations with voters and backers, nor would they need an office in their home district and travel expenses to reach it. These modest improvements would save $300 million per year.

A House member's office at present performs a good deal of "constituency service" which is not directly connected to fundraising or vote-getting. This includes the provision of information, interceding in citizens' quarrels with government agencies, facilitating the operation of government programs in the home district, and so on. This role, largely a watch-dogging one, was not foreseen by the founders since the small government machinery of their day did not interact with citizens on the scale and with the complexity of today's huge bureaucracy. It is not clear that this function is one that legislative members should serve; it has devolved upon them through the absence of other effective means of citizen service—and as an indirect way to generate contributions and votes.

A Representative House, rather than let such matters be taken over by the Senate, might institute an ombuds service, whose sole function was to expedite citizen complaints. This service could be modeled on the Legal Assistance Programs, which have been one of the great successes of recent legislative history—so successful as to earn the enmity of administration officials whose lives are made less easy by effective citizen representation.

19. The New House Would Offer Exciting Benefits to Chosen Representatives

Some people, imagining themselves to be chosen as members of the Representative House, may worry about the disruption of their lives caused by dropping their present activities and spending three years in Washington. We believe this problem could be met in large part by the following provisions.

First, the annual salaries paid to Representative House members should be large enough to represent several years' average income, and modest living quarters should be provided for those who chose to utilize them. A three-year pay totaling $210,000 would represent a windfall greater than most Americans can ever hope to receive through inheritance, business coups, insurance settlements, gambling winnings, or other rare events. If a representative saved $100,000 of this income, it would constitute a nest-egg sufficient, if invested in bonds at current rates, to generate some $10,000 per year for the rest of the person's life.

Second, legislation should provide incentives for employers to reemploy members of the House after their term in office, just as they are now obliged to give employees time off for jury duty.

Third, like present-day Congressmembers, members of the Representative House would have the option of spending part of their term at home, and could thus (though at some personal travel expense) tend to essential personal business from time to time.

This degree of disruption of personal life for 435 people seems minimal in comparison with many disrupting elements that are well established and accepted in our society. Millions of young men, either voluntarily or through the draft in the past, spend several years in military service. Thousands of people young and old join the Peace Corps and interrupt their normal stateside lives for two or three years at a stretch. Corporate executives and career military personnel routinely accept frequent relocations to distant and often not highly desirable communities as part of their normal career pattern. Training programs, college attendance, and moves to follow the job market require uprooting of millions of people from their previous lives.

None of these involve the excitement of participating in important government decisions, the development of skills in evaluating legislation, or the sense of power that would belong to members of the Representative House. We might, indeed, hope for the evolution of a new kind of citizen political figure: members of the new House with the simple eloquence of a Lincoln or the moral force of an Elizabeth Cady Stanton or Barbara Jordan—people who would rise brilliantly to the new opportunities for direct expression of the people's needs and feelings.

Many such members of the Representative House would, after their terms of office, continue as forceful defenders of the public good in their home communities, offering new vitality there; some might also decide to run for elective office. The effect would be an enrichment of the country's political life, and a welcome sense of bonding and confidence between the people and current or past occupants of House seats—in place of the present prevalent hostility and suspicion.

20. The Representative House Would Encourage Cooperation Among Members

The founders of our Republic expressed a distinct view about human behavior in the constitutional structure and in *The Federalist Papers*. Humans are divided into many groups by natural qualities, by social conditions and by changing circumstances, which gave rise to "factions." Natural qualities were God-given differences such as gender or ethnicity; women and native Americans were not suited to vote or hold office. Social conditions that create human differences were slavery, poverty, moral and physical degeneracy—additional reasons for not being allowed to vote. In addition minimum ages were established for various elected offices because social conditions determined suitability on the basis of age.

It was "changing circumstances" that most determined the political views of humans held by the founding fathers. Factions were inevitable and inherently the basic source of human conflict. Farmers were a faction in conflict with townsfolk, mountaineers were a faction opposed to coastal dwellers, and so on. Factions arose out of a human predisposition toward squabbling, greed, and self-serving behavior. The Federalist solutions were many: geographical representation in the House with short terms of office and majority voting; a bicameral legislature; an independent executive and judiciary with broad geographic bases and long-term policy responsibilities. The whole intent of the structure was to diffuse factional conflict over geography, time and social class.

Two hundred years have not changed our consensus views of human behavior very much, but they have changed slightly. Women and others are allowed to vote as we have decided that natural differences and social conditions do not create human differences of sufficient magnitude to be debilitating in the political process. Further, some of us now see factions in other terms than natural dispositions toward mutually hostile behavior. Farmers are in conflict with city folk on some issues because their differing needs and experiences have shaped their views. Farmers want irrigation from river water to supplement rain as a source of water for their crops, city folk want river water for drinking, recreation and as a transport for waste disposal. Greed is not the core issue—resource sharing, conservation, and allocation are. This kind of thinking allows us to look at conflict resolution in more manageable and optimistic terms.

Contemporary popular thinking will probably grow to favor such an approach as Americans get a chance to be comfortable with the concept. An elective legislature rewards divisiveness and encourages competition and corruption. A sortition legislature brings out the cooperative spirit and encourages socially concerned behavior.

21. Democratic Representation Will Strengthen the Republic

Some will claim that, despite the professed ideals and apparent democratic structures of American government, strong and efficient government on the imperial scale of twentieth-century America requires the existence of a powerful elite that can dominate the society. Only the members of such an elite, it is argued, can perceive long-range problems, secure expert advice, come to a consensus among themselves, and lead the mass of society to act in ways that will meet the problems, even if often at great cost. (The Trilateral Commission was an attempt to formalize such an elite role.) The present American Congress, this position holds, is a necessary evil because it gives the people the illusion of control over the government; it is tolerable to the elite because the price of managing Congress is well within the means available to the elite. But an unmanageable Representative House would hamstring long-range policy making and weaken the republic.

This view, pretending to Macchiavellian "realism," places itself outside the candid discourse of democratic societies, but it must be dealt with nonetheless. We note, first, that it presumes that the interests of the elite are rightly predominant and that the elite's definitions of problems and solutions are inherently more important than the people's. We know of no axiom to justify this position except the view that property is more important than people, and a society seeking long-term stability is ill-advised to rely on such a view.

It is likely that a government including a Representative House would develop somewhat different long-range policies than the present government produces, but policies there would be. If the differences were due principally to a more acute perception of the social costs of different policies, they might in fact strengthen the republic; they might, for instance, produce a healthier environment for its inhabitants, improve its medical delivery services, increase its literacy and its educational and technological capacities, minimize its wastefulness in military procurement, preserve its eroding crop lands, and so on. When elite spokesmen speak of "strong government," they tend to mean one with activist policies, adopted at the expense and risk of the public, which enable the government to influence international (as well as domestic) affairs for the benefit of business. We do not know whether a Representative House would be more or less jingoistic than the present House, and thus "strengthen" or "weaken" American intervention in the rest of the world. In either case, however, policies adopted could be presumed to have much greater public backing than at present. This is a kind of government strength that other nations, both friendly and hostile, would have to respect.

It has often been argued that the "weakness" of democratic societies is their divisiveness, their openness to political argument, their reluctance to give even popular rulers the power to suppress dissent and move forcefully against enemies. In its history thus far, the United States has had only mixed success in its restraint of powerful leaders bent on doubtful international adventures. If a Representative House had been in existence during the post-World War II epoch, it might have spared us most of the Korean War, the Vietnam War, the 1965 invasion of the Dominican Republic, and our involvements in Central America. Such "weakness" would have made the country's recent history, we can now see in retrospect, a much happier one, with a greater degree of internal coherence—and probably a much healthier economy.

22. The Representative House Would Not Disturb the Balance of Power

The theory of balance of power that underlies our constitutional structure assumes specific law-making, watch-dog and budget-setting functions for Congress. Congress is given a wide range of powers, from the Senate's consent in dealing with executive appointments and signing treaties to the entire Congress's power to declare war. We do not want to affect this balance unless it is clearly for the better.

The Congress of 1816 supervised a budget of $30 million, raised primarily from customs duties; in comparison the present budget is in the hundred of billions and comes to 23% of the GNP. The Congress of 1816 had 186 members, 243 employees and supervised an executive branch with 4,480 employees. Today the executive branch has 5.1 million employees, with 680,000 overseas. The 700 million acres of lands owned by the Federal government, many with valuable natural resources, are worth hundreds of billions of dollars.

The power of Congress to control or at least check the executive is always a changing balance. Under Presidents Taft and Ford, Congress established its own priorities and acted with considerable independence. Under Presidents Roosevelt and

Johnson, Congress was often a rubber stamp.

Two current issues of power balance are actively being debated. One concerns the assumption of war-making powers by the executive branch. Two major wars and numerous invasions have been carried out by the executive branch without a Congressional declaration of war.

The other concerns Congress's ongoing power to set the national budget. The executive branch has occasionally chosen to *not spend* appropriations made by Congress—a veto power that is not in the constitution. Additionally, on the same subject, the Supreme Court recently ruled against a long-standing Congressional practice of building "review hearings" into agency budgets—another reduction of Congress's power.

At present the executive proposes programs and budgets and Congress modifies them. Congress is generally too poorly organized, and sometimes too paralyzed by interest group or party conflicts, to originate either. This has not always been the case.

The American people have traditionally desired a weak central government with occasional reversal of that tendency during war time. We place far greater trust than most peoples in local government and voluntary institutions. The balance of powers was a concept designed to avoid federal tyranny and oligarchy.

The present Congress has been unsuccessful in retaining its share of constitutional power, even though it has increased its total number of employees, since the 1930s, from 1,150 to 31,800. In the 1970s it added its own economic forecasting section to cross-check that of the executive branch.

A Representative House would have several disadvantages in the battle for power against the executive, and at least one advantage, its great moral authority. The Representative House would not have many long-term members to remember and pass on to new members the tricks used by the executive to gain consent for its programs, nor would those long-term members be around to audit policies that are implemented over long periods of time (such as complex weapons systems or relations with international agencies). On the other hand, the Senate would still exist and would have many long-term members to fulfill these functions.

What would be the source of power of the new Representative House? Our elected House speaks with the authority of the interests its members are supported by: corporations and trade associations, above all, plus the unions and citizen organizations that also provide money needed for election and re-election. When members are challenged, these interests can be mobilized in defense, influencing the media and public opinion. The Congress, in an election system, is as strong as its connections.

A Representative House, like the Supreme Court, is an institution of another kind. The source of the Court's power is our allegiance to the constitution. The source of the House's authority would be a similar moral authority—rooted, like the president's own, in the nation—in the fundamental democratic concept of the consent of the governed. The ultimate power of the people behind the authority of a Representative House is the eternal possibility of rebellion and resistance. The withdrawal of consent by even a large minority may make a modern industrial society unworkable. The United States had a taste of this phenomenon during the conflict over the Vietnam War, when a substantial portion of American young people, many from elite families, turned against their fathers' war. An established Representative House would speak with what Alexander Hamilton in the *Federalist Papers* called the "irresistible force possessed by that branch of a free government which has the people on its side." In democratic societies, that is the final authority.

23. The Senate Would Remain and Represent State and Party Interests

Scholars dispute the causes of the decline in strength of American political parties since World War II. Our parties no longer maintain effective ward or county organizations capable of doing favors for numerous ordinary citizens in return for votes. Their ostensible ideological profiles, always blurred, have become increasingly indistinguishable. And as political campaigning has become less a matter of direct personal contact with potential supporters and more reliant on media advertising and manipulation, ties between politicians and the mass of voters have weakened—along with ties *among* politicians, who now tend to be more needy of money from contributors than they are of favors from colleagues. The strength of party identification among voters has declined, with markedly more cross-over voting and a massive increase in the number of people who do register and vote but call themselves independents—together with the growing numbers who neither register nor vote.

Under such circumstances, how would a Representative House affect the party structure? The parties would continue to raise funds, campaign for office, develop platforms, and reward their friends and supporters, though their national operations would now focus entirely on the presidency and the Senate. The existence of the Representative House would in time exert some indirect influence on the remaining election process, probably favoring politicians who were skillful in preparing legislation that could win approval of the House over those whose bills were uniformly rejected. That is, the new House might make the party machinery somewhat more responsive to general public needs. The threat of the extension of the sortition principle to state legislatures might also have salutary effects on state governments and party organizations.

The adoption of a Representative House, though it would weaken the sense of geographic constituency, would not significantly alter the existing geographic distribution of Representatives. States with large populations would continue to send proportionately large numbers of Representatives to Washington, and states with small populations would continue to send small numbers; geographical balance would thus be preserved. (Politically controversial problems of redistricting would be avoided, however.) Moreover, Senators would continue to be elected on a state-by-state basis, so they would go on representing the special interests of their respective states—especially the corporate interests in those states. No change would thus be likely in the national geographic balance of power because of the change to direct representation.

24. The Representative House Would Respond More Rapidly to New Problems

On the whole, we believe that a Representative House would fit in easily with the generally anti-ideological tenor of American public political life, in which party leaders and ideas are drawn toward central areas of consensus, and class differences are generally downplayed.

In one respect a Representative House can definitely be expected to increase the responsiveness of the American political system. Unlike other parliamentary democracies, we have only two parties. This arrangement is fortified by many institutional features which make entrance onto the political scene impossible for a new party except under truly revolutionary circumstances, such as prevailed at the birth of the Republican party. (At that time, neither the Democrats nor the other existing party, the Whigs, were willing to respond to the new national anti-slavery majority; the new Republican party grew up, with startling rapidity, to represent that majority—and to preside over the Civil War.)

Our two parties thus tend to split over long-standing traditional quarrels while new and pressing issues go unattended, as has happened in recent years with environmental problems of deep concern to the people. Entrance of such problems onto the national agenda is thus delayed, by contrast with parliamentary systems having a number of smaller parties—one or another of which is usually accessible to new issues and new ideas about them.

A Representative House, not being captive to the two dominant parties, could be expected to be still more flexible and open in devoting attention to new national problems—though here too, we offer no hope of a panacea, since media corporations would presumably maintain much of their present control over the perceived political agenda.

25. The Representative House Would Restore a Sense of Citizenship

The most positive result we can envision flowing from a Representative House is some restoration of the dwindling sense among ordinary Americans that they have a legitimate and honorable stake in their country—that they have been and will be listened to. The great waves of skepticism, resignation, confusion, and cynicism which sweep large masses of people as they confront the results of the arms race and the economic policies of their government would be greatly mitigated if people felt their peers had a proper share in making public policy, instead of merely being victimized by powerful interests.

The coming years will not be easy ones for ordinary Americans. The fear of nuclear annihilation is growing, and we now know that human extinction, at least in the Northern Hemisphere, could follow the nuclear-winter effects of even "minor" nuclear exchanges. The economic situation shows few credible signs of significant long-range improvement. The slow decline in real income (the amount of bread you buy with an hour's work) which began for most Americans about 1969 has left us with a lower standard of living. The prospects for rebuilding our decaying infrastructure—housing, roads, bridges, railroads, subways, water systems—seem dim, and the effects of the decay bear most heavily on ordinary people. The chemical pollution of the national environment, with the drinking water of some 40% of our population likely to be imperiled in the next decade, bears hardest on those who cannot afford bottled water or filtering systems, and on those whose workplaces and neighborhoods are most heavily contaminated with carcinogenic compounds.

In the great post-World War II expansionary period, marked injustice in the distribution of society's goods and other rewards was accepted largely because of the consistent experience that next year the whole pie, and therefore even unjustly small portions of it, would grow. In the present period, when we confront the finiteness of earth's resources and the likelihood of long-term American relative economic decline (until we and the other industrial nations reach some rough parity) many people are likely to press for more open, equal cooperative dealings in both business and government. The example of more cooperative and coherent societies adept at living within limited resources, such as Japan, Sweden, and Finland, may come to seem much more appropriate to our new situation. A Representative House would presumably be greatly more receptive to this shift in attitudes. By encouraging worker ownership, worker representation on boards of directors, and more equable distribution of income, it could ease our transition into this less comfortable era.

26. Practical Implementation Is Possible, Beginning on the State Level

Might a Representative House be adopted into the American system? Barring widespread rebellion and the adoption of a wholly new government, this would require either a constitutional amendment or an action by a constitutional convention. Is there any reason to believe, then, that Congress itself or three quarters of the states might someday come to favor a Representative House?

The prospect is far more threatening to established interests and their political friends, in terms of actual power shifts, than were previous extensions of the suffrage. Adding blacks or women to the voting rolls (except for the case of blacks in some Southern localities where they constituted a majority) brought no sudden structural changes. Moreover, it is only after blacks have had the vote (in principle) for a hundred years that important black politicians have begun to emerge; women have had the vote for sixty years before the emergence of the current "gender gap" differentiating their voting patterns from men's. The adoption of a Representative House would of course remove from power a significant number of influential persons, as well as deprive their friends and dependents throughout the county of helpful influence in Washington. This is a prospect all concerned can be expected to oppose with every political resource available to them.

Nevertheless, we believe that the idea of direct representation is not quixotic. Once it is widely understood, it will have the same overwhelming appeal to fairness and justice that motivated extensions of the suffrage. Every failure of attempts to curb the influence of money on electoral campaigns will make the idea a little less bizarre and a little more attractive. No people, and least of all Americans descended from the fiercely democratic colonists, could be expected to display lasting enthusiasm for the kind of pseudo-representation that has come to afflict us under our existing arrangements. In time, thus, sortition will seem the only reliable way to restore the voice of the people to the high councils of the republic.

Aside from intermittent attempts to reduce corruption, the defects of our electoral system have not received much concerted thought in recent years. We do not know if this is due to resignation, complacency, or simply a lack of intellectual curiosity. For example, Michael Walzer, one of our most distinguished political philosophers, recently published *Spheres of Justice: A Defense of Pluralism and Equality* (Basic Books, 1983), in which elections are not discussed at all, though the book is a thoughtful and in other respects comprehensive survey of our methods of distributing offices and goods. What makes this especially curious is that Walzer is aware of the Greek uses of sortition and of the current possibilities for using lotteries for greater fairness in such areas as the granting of jobs or grants among equally qualified candidates, but the only application of the sortition principle to politics that he can conceive is the odd notion that individual citizens might be given random chances to "pass" legislation—a notion which, of course, he properly dismisses.

Despite the novelty of the direct-representation idea at present, and the surprise that it naturally occasions when people first encounter it, we believe that like women's suffrage, legalized abortion, no-smoking sections in planes or restaurants, or mandatory recycling of cans and bottles, it can gradually gain credibility—especially through trials on the local level, where the above issues first gained acceptance. As it happens, there are 23 states that currently have an initiative process and could fairly readily vote to introduce a sortition process into the selection of their lower-house representatives. There is one legislature in the country where the adoption of sortition would produce less abrupt change than in other places. The lower house of the Oregon legislature presently has 23% women members, and only 18% lawyers. Oregon, though a nominally Republican state, has been for some decades one of the most socially innovative of the states, and if a state experiment in sortition comes, Oregon is a likely place for it.

Another state that is a possible candidate for early experimentation with direct representation is Massachusetts. It currently has an initiative process, a large lower house (160 members) and a long history of town meeting democracy on a local level. Two elements make the Massachusetts House of Representatives an interesting prospect for such a change. First, the size of the legislature has long been a publicly discussed political issue in the state, so that the relation between size and representativeness has already become a familiar question. Second, the legislature convenes in a major city, Boston, where urban newspapers regularly keep the citizenry abreast of political developments and improvements would be quickly recognized and appreciated.

The Massachusetts debate bears on the more general question of how large bodies must be (whether elected or chosen by sortition) to be, in principle, properly broad and representative. Houses of state legislatures usually have less than 100 members. Juries of 12 pseudo-randomly selected people are commonly used to weigh very serious issues. Many city and county councils are about the same size as a jury, and this size seems to have proved generally satisfactory. Therefore it is a reasonable question whether such smaller bodies could also be chosen by sortition. The answer is yes, at least where such groups would operate under conditions similar to a jury.

The reason that members of such a small group could be effective representatives has to do with the statistical nature of "representation." Any theoretical "group" is generally considered representative if its attributes are predictably within 5% of the figures for the same attributes for the whole population. The minimum size of any group that meets this requirement is determined by the magnitude of variation of the attributes in the whole population. If an attribute is known and its prevalence is great, such as the proportion of people who don't like brown drinking water or the proportion of Americans who can understand the word "STOP" on a street sign, then a very small randomly selected group can reliably be used to represent the whole population on those issues. If the question were "Would you allow 50% more dirt in your water if the water bill dropped by 25%?" then ten randomly selected people would be enough to know the answer. Similarly if the question put to a small group was whether to use a round sign that said "PAUSE," we would get a reliable decision.

Juries are reliable for this reason. We assume that basic moral values are fairly similar for all people in our culture; therefore twelve people asked to judge unanimously whether some matter of alleged fact is "beyond a shadow of doubt" can achieve the same result as the whole population, given the same evidence and instructions. The same principle applies to small legislative bodies. If we required unanimous consent from a randomly selected twelve-member city council, on issues that were widely agreed upon by the population, we would get reliable results.

However, many issues faced by legislative bodies require the balancing of uncertain claims and interests, and uniform assumptions about values do not prevail on many political questions. It seems likely, therefore, that direct-representation bodies on local or state levels would gain greater public acceptance if they numbered at least 25 persons. The statistics of sortition would ensure that such a body was substantially more representative than existing smaller bodies.

If we evolve toward a society in which fairness and equality are important values—and prospects of economic and resource scarcity may loosen the hold of traditional individualist, competitive values—sortition may gradually seem a normal way of distributing many goods, including political power. On local levels, rotating leadership has been used in feminist groups, academic departments, small business collectives, affinity groups in protest movements, neighborhood organizations, and so on. Even though sortition may not be seriously considered for a legislative body for many years, experiments of this kind will gradually familiarize people with the principle. Moreover, the very existence of the concept offers a liberation from traditional notions and a kind of standard against which to judge our elected bodies as the years pass.

There is also a charming peculiarity of the Representative House that should greatly appeal to the American gambling spirit. Tens of millions of Americans presently wager large sums in casinos, lotteries, legal and illegal track and sport betting, and so on. The Representative House proposed here would offer to 145 people each year the chance to become rich, famous, and important beyond their wildest expectations. The odds of this happening to any individual during an eligible lifetime from 25 to say 75 would be slightly better than one in twenty-five thousand. Such appealing odds might greatly contribute to popular acceptance of the sortition principle. (A corollary to this statistic is the fact that after the scheme had been in effect for 25 years, every town or neighborhood with 20,000 people or so would contain one person who had served in the Congress. Presumably most of these would become valuable community assets through their experiences in Washington.)

The arrival of direct representation on the political agenda will set off a lengthy and fierce political struggle, but it is an idea that, once understood, will refuse to go away. Since we can hardly expect the existing House to vote itself out of existence, the impetus for the necessary constitutional amendment will ultimately have to come from the people operating though their state governments. That such forces can have an impact on the required scale is clear from the recent effort to compel Congress to adopt a balanced-budget amendment—or, if Congress should balk, to force the calling of a constitutional convention. This process is instructive as a matter of democratic principle. Our system still offers ways for the people to make their views heard, and they do not suffer infractions of this power lightly. In time, they may well conclude that the best solution to the unrepresentativeness of our present compromised legislators is to establish a Representative House that would provide, at last, the "transcript" of the people spoken of by the founders.

Responses

We solicited responses to the above text from a wide range of persons with varying political perspectives and experience.

We are most grateful to those who were willing to comment, for inclusion in the book, on this initial publication of our proposal. Since we believe that the sortition principle should be of interest to all people with a concern for democratic government, we hope to include additional comments from still other points of view in a future edition. —E.C. and M.P.

George Dean

The limitations of our so-called "representative government" are eloquently demonstrated by the fate of presidential candidate Jesse Jackson. Clearly the most articulate and charismatic of the candidates, he could never generate the millions necessary for a statewide television campaign, due in large measure to his commitment to unpopular issues.

Today we have a policy of one million dollars per candidate that nullifies the U.S. Supreme Court's historic "one man, one vote" decision.

Over the last decade, disenfranchised minorities have strongly supported a wide range of Common Cause-type political reforms. All had potential but the net result of this decade of reform is that only millionaires and those in gerrymandered districts are free from the financial pressures of political action committees (PACs).

Equally disturbing, the economic status of blacks has declined and the vast majority of our representatives, increasingly beholden to PACs, care little and do less.

From the perspective of this nation's black population, there appears to be little risk and much potential from an experiment with a citizen legislature that could draw one quarter of its representatives from our nation's fifty-nine million poor and near-poor.

George Dean is the President of the California Urban League and the Sacramento Urban League.

Robert Gnaizda

Few who dare to closely examine our political process have any doubt as to its potential for corruption, ineffectiveness and exorbitant costs. Most alarming, those who do not examine our political process closely have drawn the same conclusions. This is why a majority of Americans *refuse* to vote and it is why the so-called "best and brightest" are seldom elected to legislatures and almost never chosen for leadership roles.

Talented political reformers, such as Common Cause, have increasingly been successful in appearing to reform the process. In reality they have failed. The reformers, in their zeal, have ignored a key fact of life: the talents of reformers rarely exceed the cunning and ambition of those they seek to reform.

As a result of the last decade of reform, which has produced frequent one-million-dollar local legislative races and an abundance of multi-million- dollar PACs, an increasing number of Americans have accepted the fact that modest reforms do not work. It is why I support, on a state level, having one house of a bicameral legislature chosen from our citizens at large, at least as a pilot program for one decade. This will provide us with sufficient time to determine the validity of the thesis developed by the authors of this book while still allowing legislative and executive oversight from the governor and the other house.

With a few modest restrictions on citizen eligibility, I believe the integrity of the citizen legislature would exceed that of any legislature in America. As for the intelligence of its *leaders*, they

Robert Gnaizda of Public Advocates is an attorney who won women the right to be police officers, blacks the right to be in firedepartments and Filippinos to be CPAs. He removed the legal limit on savings accounts for senior citizens and released federal dairy surpluses for the poor to eat.

would clearly be at least as intelligent and would be far more effective since the leaders would be free from corrupt political pressures.

The modest restrictions on eligibility for this citizen legislature would include limiting service to those 21 to 70, require at least two prior registrations to vote as a sign of interest in the political process, set a minimum English literacy standard, require a six-week professional training course, and permit the citizen legislature to evict any of its unqualified members for cause.

A key criticism of a citizen legislature is that it is similar to the jury system and the jury system has failed. The citizen legislature, although modeled after a jury system, contains none of its defects. Offering a salary approximately three times the average family income, and a four-year term of office, 99% of all Americans who are selected would undoubtedly serve. In contrast, the majority of our citizens and 99% of our leaders do not serve on juries because lawyers consider them "too qualified or knowledgeable."

Moreover, whatever the frailties of the jury system may be, and they are many, the vast majority of Americans have always preferred to have important decisions affecting their lives or property decided by juries rather than by politically appointed judges, many of whom were once legislators.

Loni Hancock

Traveling in Greece for a month last year, I also became intrigued with the notion of a randomly selected governing body, and whether an idea that worked brilliantly for several centuries in a small, pre-industrial city state can be adapted to the needs of a huge polyglot post-industrial nation.

America's democratic system for choosing representatives and defining our community life also worked brilliantly for several centuries. It is now trying to adapt to a basic contradiction—unlimited private dollars which confound the democratic selection process to the point where, as George Orwell put it, "all are equal, but some are more equal than others." When "some are more equal than others" the game is rigged, and it is understandable why the unequal players opt out of the game through non-participation or disrupt the game with violence. When "some are more equal than others" the social contract of a democracy is threatened.

The idea of a lottery is at first thought absurd, and at second thought obvious. It raises fundamental questions in new ways. It ought to be part of the public debate on retaining a vigorous democracy in the United States. It might work.

I have two major questions about a lottery:

Leadership: Granted that present legislators are no more perspicacious than the rest of us, the fact remains that many of them are *there* for many years. We live in an extraordinarily complicated world in which "knowing the details" of an issue or a parliamentary procedure can make all the difference.

I see no way for persons serving one three-year term to

Loni Hancock, who was formerly an elected city council member in Berkeley, California, is now the co-director of Initiatives for Campaign Reform, 680 Beach Street, Suite 462, San Francisco, CA 94109.

become conversant with the nuances of issues and procedure, develop alternatives, build a public constituency for them (which requires understanding of media and the skills to use it) and oversee implementation of a new program or policy. Rare individuals may be able to have some impact in one issue area, but the long-term leadership will come from the Senate which, in this proposal, is still elected on the basis of money.

Randomly selected delegates in the lower house will rely heavily on the three-month training period to become minimally conversant with issues and legislative process. This simply means that the trainers (bureaucrats) will have enormous power to define alternatives by providing information to people with few alternative resources. In this proposal, the trainers can practically define the national options. And, who will train the trainers?

The Jury Analogy: The lottery system as proposed is essentially voluntary. There is the option of simply collecting the salary and going on with one's daily life. Our present jury system is compulsory. Even so, and even though the term of service is rarely more than one month, it has had problems achieving representative participation.

I recently served on a jury in Alameda County Superior Court on which I was the only "professional." All the other doctors, lawyers, accountants, etc. whose "numbers came up" pleaded hardship and were excused by the judge.

There is a real danger that a non-compulsory lottery system would have such a high non-attendance rate that it would not be representative. Even a compulsory system like our jury system might have so many "excused absences" that the same result would occur.

There are many reasons for reluctance to set aside three years to serve as a legislator. Some people simply passionately want to do something else—whether write a novel or make a million dollars. And what about families? Would spouses be helped to

70

relocate in Washington, DC? What about moving children, schools, etc.? It may be possible to mitigate these problems—they need more thought.

A major flaw, I think, is that the lottery system, as proposed, would leave power in the hands of bureaucrats and those elected and re-elected to the upper house through undue influence of money. The lottery should be accompanied by traditional campaign reform. If the total system is to work, it requires a Senate elected on the basis of ideas and leadership qualities, not money.

Initiatives for Campaign Reform, a non-profit research and advocacy group, has concluded that a real level playing field for ideas requires three things: limits on the amount of each contribution to election campaigns; limits on how much a campaign can spend; and citizen financing of campaigns. There are many ways to implement citizen financing. After a year-long study, ICR recommends matching small contributions (under $500) from individuals with money from a public fund.

Citizen financing is controversial and absolutely essential. It is the key to an elected legislature that works for the public good rather than for large campaign contributors. ICR's study found that two thirds of the contributions to the average legislative campaign in California now come from political action committees (PACs), banks and corporations. Only 14% comes from individuals. Only 9% is small contributions (under $100). Given these percentages, simply limiting contribution size won't work. For example, PACs can divide, with each sub-PAC making the maximum contribution; checks can be "bundled" and delivered at the same time by a lobbyist to make sure the legislator "gets the message," etc.

For real independence to vote their conscience, an *alternative* to special-interest money is necessary, and that alternative source of money can only be the citizens-at-large. The *polis* as the Greeks called it.

71

ICR is working to achieve public support for citizen financing of elections. We found that by eliminating even one of the numerous tax loopholes and preferences now enacted to appease big contributors, citizen financing would more than pay for itself. We have been told that we are "too idealistic" and that the special interests whose power is based on money are so entrenched in our country that real democracy will not be possible again. We don't believe it. To believe it is to give up on the best hope of achieving a world in which people matter—a world that has been struggling to be achieved from the time of the Greek city states, through the Renaissance and the founding of national democracies in the Age of Reason. We've come too far and too many have worked too hard to allow the "interested few" to take over our democracy by buying the process by which we choose the makers of public decisions.

ICR plans to promote our recommendations for all elective offices in the state of California. We applaud the entry of the lottery concept into the debate, however.

If we devise ways to iron out the problems of de facto bureaucratic takeover, and the voluntary-compulsory conundrum, a sortition lower house would be a friendly addition to the alternatives under consideration. It can only be helpful to have democracy's roots and premises in the forefront of our thinking as we explore fundamental solutions instead of tinkering with the symptoms.

Malcolm Margolin

The present system of electing representatives is certainly flawed and abused. But it has survived for a couple of hundred years, demonstrating surprising resilience, and before chucking it for an untried idea, I would suggest that a few preliminary experiments with sortition might be advisable. The medical profession, for example, is dreadfully and perniciously undemocratic, dominated by wealthy white males with (I seriously believe) socially harmful consequences. Therefore let us first use sortition to choose doctors (or, if we want to be very cautious, candidates to medical school). That way we can be assured that the doctors of the future will reflect the society in a most exact transcript, which will undoubtedly greatly improve the quality of medical services. We might also choose our dentists, judges, plumbers, engineers, police officers, and architects this way—perhaps giving them all tenures of three years in their assigned professions lest they become jaded and corrupt.

If the above proposition appears preposterous, it is because we recognize that to be an excellent doctor, dentist, judge, plumber, engineer, police officer, or architect one must have aptitude, interest, intelligence, and the willingness and time to cultivate professional skills. No matter how deep my democratic feelings and my commitment to civil rights, I would not entrust my body to a group of doctors chosen by sortition from the general populace, nor would I trust the nation to a group of legislators chosen the same way. Legislating, I believe, is (at least ideally—and this is what we are talking about, *ideal* forms of government) a pursuit that demands a high level of skill and

Malcolm Margolin is the author of *East Bay Out*, *The Ohlone Way*, and *The Way We Lived*. He is also the founder of Heyday Books.

experience. Perhaps the current system of electing our representatives fails us in this regard—although it is at least arguable that those who get elected to public office have assembled a staff, run a campaign, raised and handled huge sums of money, gained the support of diverse elements in the society, made some convincing speeches, and otherwise demonstrated at least some ability to exercise the arts of leadership. If, as you suggest (and I fully agree), people chosen this way are not skilled or responsible enough, this is a grievous defect in the present system. But it is not, to my mind, an indication that such qualities are unnecessary, and I do not see how it benefits the nation to devise a new system that even further devalues aptitude, skill, and experience.

The most severe drawback to government by lottery—one that makes it in my eyes totally unacceptable—is that it cuts people off from the opportunity to vote for their congressional representatives. Voting is the major (often the only) political act in most people's lives. However imperfect the process, millions of citizens examine the actions of their congressional representatives every two years and vote. It is this specific citizen endorsement—not any abstract idea of democratic representation—that gives the government its legitimacy and insures citizen acceptance of the government's decisions. I am quite fearful of any process which cuts millions of people off from participating in their own government—cuts the bonds that connect the ruled with those who rule.

This connection is particularly important on the congressional level. The elections of president and senators are huge and seemingly abstract—almost like distant media events. One feels very little personal effectiveness in such situations. To speak for myself, my only direct connection to the federal government in Washington is through my congressman. I have met him and I know several of his staff members. I have contributed to his campaign, and have supported and en-

74

dorsed him. He is my one and only link with Washington. Through him and his office I feel that I have a voice in the legislative process. If I disagree with a particular bill, I feel that I can write to him or call one of his staff members, and I feel that my opinions will at least get a hearing. Sure, the situation is far from ideal, but it is through him—and only through him—that I feel some small (but all-important) sense of influence over the forces that run my life. Without this linkage, what power do I have? I have never met either of my senators nor do I know the president. Take away the elected congressman and you further alienate millions of people like myself from their government—creating a greater impersonalizing and distancing that I think is terribly dangerous for the nation and would spell the end of the democratic process.

Despite the populist rhetoric, I find your entire proposal to be disturbingly contemptuous of the people. Like it or not, the present congress (which you obviously despise) was elected by large numbers of the very people whose wisdom and good judgment you extol. I agree that its composition is not even an approximate transcript of the population at large, but I wonder (I am not certain) whether this does not represent the will of the people. It is at least worth considering whether the people in electing the kinds of congressional candidates they do have deliberately chosen not to be governed by their barber, their accountant, the unemployed derelict who hangs around the neighborhood liquor store, or the nice lady who runs the cosmetic counter at Woolworth's. Perhaps the reason they elect the people they do is not because they are stupid or duped, but because they *want* to be ruled by people whom they perceive (however mistakenly) as successful, powerful, and capable, and in our culture these people tend to be wealthy, white males often with a background in law. Such people do not represent my own ideas of excellence, and I personally believe most of the choices made by our electorate are wrong.

But I am deeply enough committed to the democratic process to believe that the rights of people to choose their own leaders must be respected and defended, and (however grave its shortcomings) is vastly preferable to your patronizing idea of having the choice made for them by the laws of random selection.

Beyond its theoretical shortcomings, I'm afraid that I find the idea of government by lottery to be (to put it bluntly) utterly silly and unworkable. I read, for example, your description of what a debate might be among the assembled and stalwart yeomanry, how responsibly and intelligently they will conduct themselves, yielding to one another, listening acutely to arguments, weighing decisions. It is possible, I believe, and without too much exaggeration, to picture a different kind of scene. Among these people, given the laws of random selection, will be a few who will be talking to themselves out loud. Several dozen will be outright alcoholics and there will probably be a heroin addict or two. I can picture the debate over a bill—let us say a bill of some complexity dealing with international trade. Most of those listening to the debates have not read a book since high school, and simply do not have the patience or the concentration or the background to follow difficult and tedious arguments for very long. In the old days, when the House of Representatives was an elected body, House members had staffs who could study issues and prepare reports. But most of the members of the sortition House do not have the ability to choose talented staffs, direct them, and use the information generated by them. In addition, most of the members are having grave personal problems, their lives in total disarray caused by a sudden influx of money that they don't know how to handle, a change of occupation, a move to a distant city, and separation from family and friends. In fact, personal problems are causing such stress that most of the new House members cannot concentrate very effectively on anything.

Yet the debate goes on. We first hear from the Jesus caucus, an especially strong, numerous, and well organized body of the new House, whose members, one after the other, argue that prayer and a firm belief in God will solve the problem at hand. They are convinced, in fact, that they were not chosen by chance at all, but by the hand of God to lead the nation on the path of righteousness. Then comes Old Gertie, the bag lady, who sees every issue as still another example of how the Communists are poisoning the drinking water with fluoride as part of the conspiracy to drive her crazy and cheat her of her rightful place as queen of Rumania. Meanwhile the three prostitutes are parading their wares on the floor, much to the hooting and delight of the truck-driver caucus who are listening to radios on the House floor and drinking beer. As for the more intelligent, quiet, and potentially dedicated people, they have long been driven out by the sheer exasperation and tedium of the proceedings. If anything gets done, it will be through the efforts of the permanent staff—who in this situation of chaos and continually changing membership will be the only ones who know how to get things done, and who in the final analysis will be the ones who will actually rule the House—assuming that the House is by this time worth ruling at all.

To counter this possibility, you continually point to the success of the jury system, but the differences between a jury system and government by lottery are profound. A jury consists of only twelve people. These twelve are chosen rather carefully—with prosecutor, defense attorney, and judge all having the right to sift through and eliminate candidates. The questions the jury must decide are rather limited—generally only a single question of right or wrong in a specific instance and within the framework of a well articulated body of law and precedent—and in this decision they are guided by a judge who explains carefully what they can and cannot consider. A jury might be in session for two days, five days, or even weeks in deliberating this single and well defined issue, and even

77

then its decision may be appealed and overruled if it is felt that they have overstepped their bounds. This is qualitatively different from throwing hundreds of people randomly chosen into a room, with huge numbers of issues (some only vaguely defined) that they will have to consider each day, all without careful guidance.

These are some of my major objections to the idea of government by lottery. I have many other objections, and in fact I find myself taking issue with just about every point you raise. I do not, for example, think a randomly chosen governing body would be as free from corruption as you imagine—far from it. I suspect many people chosen to serve will shirk their destinies, just as they shirk the far less onerous duties of serving on a jury today. In fact I suspect the more experienced and accomplished the person is in his or her own personal life, the more likely that person would be to avoid serving. In fact, I'm sorry to admit that the only value I have thus far derived from considering your arguments for a government by lottery is that the more I delve into it the better the present (admittedly wretched) form of government seems.

Mario Obledo

Our nation, which includes 49 million blacks and Hispanics, or a population larger than 90% of the member countries of the United Nations, does not presently have any Hispanic or black U.S. Senators.

This situation has caused many minority leaders and the minority community to question the fundamental fairness and future of our so-called "representative" government. How, they ask, can government be representative when most governmental bodies do not include persons from the two largest ethnic and racial communities in America, in any significant numbers.

Thus, we see much merit to a citizen legislature. Surely, some of its members, free from financial and political retaliation, will strive for and perhaps achieve the greatness not duplicated since the era of our founding fathers. I have no doubt whatsoever that such a legislative assembly would do a marvelous job.

Mario Obledo is the National President of the League of United Latin American Citizens (LULAC), the nation's largest Hispanic membership organization, and former Secretary of Health and Welfare for the State of California (1975-1982).

Mark Satin

There's a huge gap between the political visions of "alternative" thinkers and activists, and the practical political ideas we tend to present to the general public.

Our visions are, quite often, rich and compelling. But our policy ideas are, too often, warmed-over liberalism. Wooden and "correct" and who gives a damn.

The genius of Callenbach and Phillips's book is that they've taken a key alternative vision ("let the people decide") and translated it into an eminently sensible, practical and realizable proposal, *without stripping it of its system-transcending core.*

Thanks guys. The trouble is, that's not enough—not nearly enough.

Living in Washington, you quickly realize that political ideas are a dime a dozen. Even good political ideas. Getting them adopted is the real political challenge. Another two years here and I might write, "Getting them adopted is the only thing."

What is the constituency that will fight for your ideas? Why will it fight for *your* ideas, instead of the hundreds of other ideas now going begging for people's attention and commitment? What organizations can we count on to mobilize that constituency?

Mark Satin is the author of *New Age Politics* and the founder and editor of the newsletter *New Options* (P.O. Box 19324, Washington, DC 20036—$25.00 per year).

Charlene Spretnak

When I tell people of the Callenbach-Phillips proposal, they invariably laugh or smile skeptically. My own initial reaction was the same. But the interesting thing is that no one laughs for very long once he or she starts thinking it through.

My response to the proposal addresses points of agreement, suggested changes, and suggested additions.

I believe Callenbach and Phillips are correct to propose structural change in our selection of lawmakers rather than merely trying to fine-tune the present system, the inequities of which have actually been worsened by some of the recent reforms. First and foremost is the problem that our federal senators and representatives are bought. In this era of extremely expensive media-oriented campaigns, the answer to "Who gets to go to Washington?" is that old saw: "Them that's got the gold gets." In a rightfully disturbing article titled "What's Wrong with Congress?" (*The Atlantic,* December 1984), Gregg Easterbrook cites findings by the Congress Watch organization that representatives who sponsored the milder of two versions of the Superfund bill for the cleanup of toxic wastes, favored by business, averaged $4,784 in contributions from chemical-company PACs; those who sponsored the strict version averaged $532 from such companies. In addition to Congressional voting being influenced by large campaign contributions, there is the problem that our lawmakers must continually hustle campaign funding, especially in the House with elections ev-

Charlene Spretnak is co-author of *Green Politics: The Global Promise* (Dutton), which she wrote with Fritjof Capra. She is also editor of *The Politics of Women's Spirituality* (Anchor/Doubleday) and is a cofounder of the Committees of Correspondence (P.O. Box 40040, St. Paul, MN 55104), a national, regionally based political organization that has kinship with Green parties around the world.

ery two years. Once in a while I read interviews with freshman representatives who admit they are so consumed by attracting enough donations to pay off old campaign debts and to accumulate a sufficient amount for the next election that they simply do not have time to do a good job.

Callenbach and Phillips are also correct in noting that our present system of representation is clearly not very representative. Who goes to Congress now? Largely white, upper-middle-class males whose appearance, voice, and mannerisms work well with media demands. These men have similar educations, similar class experiences, similar priorities—and gender-role conditioning and bonding that influence their perspectives. It warms my feminist heart to think that the Callenbach-Phillips proposal would result in 51% of our House representatives being women and in all classes, ethnic groups, and races having true representation.

Citizens who oppose measures to achieve gender balance in Congress might do well to recall the words of one of the Founding Mothers, Abigail Adams. In her famous "Remember the Ladies" letter written to her husband, John Adams, at the Second Continental Congress in 1776, she observed: "If particular care and attention are not paid to the Ladies, we are determined to foment a Rebellion, and will not hold ourselves bound to obey any Laws in which we have no voice or Representation."

A secondary benefit of random selection from the populace is that Americans might actually insist on a high quality of public education: would we want to be governed by people lacking a sense of history, critical thinking and communication skills, ecological wisdom, "science literacy," global responsibility, and knowledge of various economic systems (especially a steady-state, decentralized, community-based version of capitalism!)?

Not only are different kinds of people missing from Congress today, but so are different kinds of political thinking beyond the A-to-B gamut of Republican and Democrat. In my research on the Green parties of Western Europe, I discovered that they have won seats at the federal level only in countries that have proportional representation: Belgium and West Germany.

One of the key principles of Green politics—in addition to decentralization of economic and political power, ecological wisdom, social responsibility (globally as well as locally), post-patriarchal values, and nonviolence—is "participatory democracy." The notion of selecting representatives is still maintained in such a system, but the grassroots level has more decision-making power and hence more active involvement than with the more hierarchical "representative democracy." Among the effects of stronger citizen participation—either within the two giant parties or within a few smaller, new parties, or both—would be a broader range of reflection on solutions to the problems we face as a society.

To some Americans the notion of local, state, and federal legislative bodies being comprised of representatives from small, innovative parties as well as the two giants would be a welcome change. (If we adopted the European threshhold of requiring five percent of the total vote as the minimum for winning representation, there would not be a plethora of tiny, "lunatic fringe" parties in our legislative bodies. Even five percent is hard to win; John Anderson's ambitious campaign in 1980 won only seven percent of the total national vote.) Most Americans, however, distrust ideologies and would probably never support a constitutional amendment for proportional representation so that the political debate in our country could be expanded. Random selection would do that, in a way that is familiar because of its similarity to jury duty.

I suggest changing the proposal from purely random selection to drawing from a volunteer pool. After much ado it would amount to that anyway since it is impossible to conscript people to force them to move to Washington for three years. Many citizens would get out of it by citing the same kinds of extenuating circumstances that excuse one from jury duty. (Of course, the real reasons would not be stated publicly: husbands who are threatened by the thought of their wives being powerful figures for three years; wives who refuse to give up three years of their lives to play the role of "public wife of Mr. Congressman"; spouses of both sexes who refuse to uproot themselves and their children from their community in trade for the cynical, competitive ambiance of our nation's capital.)

Having a voluntary pool would eliminate the many Americans who simply do not care about politics, but would include all those wonderfully feisty and committed citizens who run the PTAs, the Cub Scout troops, the church groups, the ethnic clubs, the environmental protection efforts, and so forth. I admit that this method would lack the inherent balance of purely random selection, but the Federal Elections Commission, or whichever agency would handle the task, could issue periodic reports encouraging more citizens of various categories to register so that their percentage in the pool would match their percentage in the general population. (The Commission might have to announce, for example, that they needed more Hispanic housewives—and fewer lawyers.)

Americans would rightfully distrust the idea of totally inexperienced representatives making decisions for us at the national and international levels. (Most freshman representatives have some political experience behind them, even if it's only years of service as a political hack in their district.) Hence the second change I suggest is that federal representatives be selected from the national pool of former state senators and state representatives, who were chosen for those one-time, three-year terms from an open volunteer pool in their states.

The question arises as to why selection for the U.S. Senate should not also be reformed in this way, as it has more power than the House and is plagued with the same problems of financing extremely costly campaigns, owing favors to monied interests, and functioning largely as a privileged, white men's club. I suppose Callenbach and Phillips's intention is to assuage fears concerning anything new by maintaining a large portion of the old system.

The additions I suggest are based on reforms proposed at the end of Gregg Easterbrook's article: limit legislators' outside income (no more $5000 and $10,000 "honoraria" for giving a talk to a group); ban lobbyists from the premises of Capitol Hill; require attendance in Washington for three quarters of the year (hectic flying back and forth almost every week for continual campaigning would no longer be necessary) and expect legislators to spend most of the summer quarter meeting with citizen groups in their areas. Easterbrook also documents the hugely inefficient tangle of overlapping committees and subcommittees that has evolved in the House and Senate since the seniority system was abandoned in 1975. Apparently, everyone in Congress decided to be chair of *something*. (Easterbrook calls it the "535-ring circus that is Congress.") Switching to the one-time, three-year terms suggested by Callenbach and Phillips would afford an opportunity to radically streamline the committee system without returning to the old system, which concentrated entrenched power in the hands of a few very senior legislators. A new seniority system could be adopted such that each committee (their total number would be combined and reduced) would be chaired by a third-year legislator who had served on that committee throughout her or his term.

Am I ready to advocate adopting the Callenbach-Phillips proposal, with my changes and additions, for the House of Representatives as soon as possible? Nope. There are too many unknowns. But the idea makes enough sense that I do think we should try random selection (from a pool of volunteers) for the lower house of state governments in as many states as are willing to go along with the experiment. The citizenry could observe the results and decide whether the new system should be expanded to the federal level, altered, or abandoned. If the new system were to be expanded to the Congressional level after the test period in several states, all states would be obliged to adopt it by a certain date so that the national pool of experienced, randomly selected legislators would be fed from the entire country.

I wish to thank several friends for discussions of the Callenbach-Phillips proposal and responses to my ideas. In particular, my ol' college chum Michael Koetting convinced me of the need for volunteer pools; I then played with combining that idea with the need for experience in our federal legislators and came up with the notion of a national pool of former state legislators, who had been randomly selected from volunteer pools. John Powell kindly delivered an eloquent argument for the need to reform selection of Senators as well as Representatives.

Hon. John Vasconcellos

"If you ask me, 'Why should not the people make their own laws?' I need only ask you, 'Why should the people not write their own plays?' They cannot. It is much easier to write a good play than to make good law. And there are not a hundred men in the world who can write a play good enough to stand the daily wear and tear as long as a law must." —Shaw

Shaw's comment may reflect the predictable bias of an elected politician after reading the reforms proposed by Callenbach and Phillips. After all, as a tenth-term California assemblyman and chairman of the influential Ways and Means Committee, who would expect me to embrace a political reform that would throw me out of office? Yet I cite Shaw in this instance with some regret.

I wish everyone could write a play; I wish everyone could create effective law. Obviously, for myriad reasons, such is not the case.

Reading *A Citizen Legislature,* I found myself pulled between the ideal of a full, literal democracy, where everyone is interested, partakes and contributes, and the reality of our republican form of government, where imperfect elected officials serve an often disinterested and suspicious electorate. But it is the tension between the ideal and the real that fuels innovation and improvement, whether in government, science or art, so I can honestly embrace many of the proposals in *A Citizen Legislature* even if I cannot push for their enactment.

The authors claim that resistance to their sortition solution comes from "an attachment to hierarchy and a lack of trust in

John Vasconcellos, who has served in the California State Assembly for two decades, is now chairman of the Committee on Ways and Means.

the people themselves." Granted, there is truth here. I suspect many people would be loathe to abolish our republican form of government that has served them so well—some because the status quo suits them, others for lack of a better idea. I also think there would be a widespread reluctance to put government into the hands of an arbitrary collection of "the people"— many of whom lack the necessary expertise, education and ability to perform the massive responsibility of governing.

Yet ironically, the authors' proposal itself constructs but a new hierarchy and does so on the basis of a cynical lack of trust in the people elected by the people.

I do not share the authors' presumptuous lack of trust in elected officials. Neither do I distrust the public. For twenty years I have based my public political career on my belief in the inherent goodness of the individual. That belief, however, does not necessarily translate into the confidence that because people are good they are suitably gifted to govern.

Even so, the Callenbach-Phillips proposal intrigues me because it echoes the themes of self-empowerment I have always preached. For example, my admiration for the liberation politics of Paolo Friere's *Pedagogy of the Oppressed* allows me to endorse the authors' earnest and creative thinking. But as the solution to our admittedly imperfect political system, I cannot support it.

The problematic question the authors' proposal raises is: do people generally know what is best for them? That question can be argued interminably. Regardless how you answer, however, you immediately face an equally troublesome quandary: assuming the need for, and the existence of, some centralized form of government, would could/would most people accomplish in working for three years in the bureaucratic maze of a mammoth institutional government?

I don't know, but I suspect very little.

The bureaucrats and staff people who really understand the ins and outs of any political system don't leave every three years. They stay on for careers. It takes several years to learn the ropes and the issues before anyone can become a force in any government, just like in any job of import. Continuity, camaraderie and trust are built up over time, not upon the oath of office.

No one would argue that elected politicians are more trustworthy or diligent than many of their constituents. But again, I think it unfair and cynical to presume they are less.

I take pride in my office, my integrity and the job I do. And after ten terms in the California Legislature I can vouch for most of my colleagues. Yes, I've seen undue influence. I've seen irresponsible campaigns and poor job performance. But the rule rather than the exception is men and women sacrificing time, careers and financial gain to serve in government, all the while criticized and held in suspicion.

Most people serving as elected officials today are highly educated professional people with skills that would serve them well in the private sector. Let's not be too quick to write off the dedication and hard work that leads to victory in open elections. On the other hand, let's not write off challenging reforms, such as those offered by Callenbach and Phillips.

Without the luxury of space for detail, I can only opine that the authors' proposals are simplistic, unwieldy and unrealistic. Nonetheless, I think it wise to pay attention to their criticisms and I do. As T. Burke once said, "A disposition to preserve and an ability to improve, taken together, would be my standard of a statesman."

Acknowledgments

In the course of preparing this book, we have received essential support from many people, often in the form of impassioned objections to which, in the course of excited conversation, new solutions arose. Though the final form of the text represents solely the authors' own views, we are especially grateful to Greta Alexander, Walter T. Anderson, Benjamin Barber, Ellen Gnaizda, Robert Gnaizda, Allen Graubard, Tommy Hargadon, Lynn Hirshman, Nan Hohenstein, Paul Kaufman, Christine Leefeldt, Deanne Marquardt, Malcolm Margolin, Frances Peavey, Richard Register, Michael Rossman, and Lee Swenson. We also reiterate here our gratitude to the people who took the time to prepare their thoughtful printed responses to the proposal. No new political idea grows in isolation; its refinement, like its application, must inevitably be a social process.

This book was written on a Kaypro 10 with Wordstar, typeset in Palatino by Lexis Press of San Francisco and printed by Edwards Bros. in Ann Arbor, Michigan. The first printing of 2,000 copies cost $2,700.

The book is owned by a partnership with the two authors as the majority investors and four friends as additional supporters.

INDIVIDUAL ORDER FORM

Clear Glass
Box 256
Bodega, CA 94922
Please send me __ copies of A CITIZEN LEGISLATURE. I enclose
$6.00 per copy (postage and handling included).

Name _____

Street _____

City, State, Zip _____